"No one gets caught up in the holidays like I do. Talk about frenzy! But Anita's hilarious spin on the holidays is enough to make even me look forward to the 'jolly' season. We'll be adding this to the required reading for the staff."

— Mrs. Claus, wife of Santa

"Anita Renfroe's outrageous humor and insightful observations on life bring mirth to the mind and warmth to the soul. *A Purse-Driven Christmas* will make the holidays merrier and your step a bit lighter this season."

— Ellie Kay, conference speaker;
best-selling author of *Kisses of Sunshine for Moms*

"I should have known Anita Renfroe could make even the grinch in me laugh uncontrollably, stuff the commercial nonsense in the attic, and drag out childhood wonder again. *A Purse-Driven Christmas* is the gift every girlfriend wants!"

— Virelle Kidder, conference speaker;
author of *Donkeys Still Talk*

a purse-driven christmas

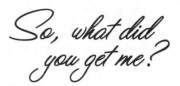

So, what did you get me?

Anita Renfroe

NAVPRESS®

BRINGING TRUTH TO LIFE

OUR GUARANTEE TO YOU

We believe so strongly in the message of our books that we are making this quality guarantee to you. If for any reason you are disappointed with the content of this book, return the title page to us with your name and address and we will refund to you the list price of the book. To help us serve you better, please briefly describe why you were disappointed. Mail your refund request to: NavPress, P.O. Box 35002, Colorado Springs, CO 80935.

NavPress
P.O. Box 35001
Colorado Springs, Colorado 80935

The Navigators is an international Christian organization. Our mission is to reach, disciple, and equip people to know Christ and to make Him known through successive generations. We envision multitudes of diverse people in the United States and every other nation who have a passionate love for Christ, live a lifestyle of sharing Christ's love, and multiply spiritual laborers among those without Christ.

NavPress is the publishing ministry of The Navigators. NavPress publications help believers learn biblical truth and apply what they learn to their lives and ministries. Our mission is to stimulate spiritual formation among our readers.

Published in association with the literary agency of Alive Communications, Inc., 7680 Goddard Street, Suite 200, Colorado Springs, CO 80920 (www.alivecommunications.com).

NAVPRESS, BRINGING TRUTH TO LIFE, and the NAVPRESS logo are registered trademarks of NavPress. Absence of ® in connection with marks of NavPress or other parties does not indicate an absence of registration of those marks.

ISBN 1-57683-898-6

Cover design by DeAnna Pierce, Bill Chiaravalle, Brand Navigation, LLC, www.brandnavigation.com
Cover photos by Brand X Pictures, The Image Bank
Creative Team: Terry Behimer, Arvid Wallen, Traci Mullins, Cara Iverson, Pat Reinheimer

Some of the anecdotal illustrations in this book are true to life and are included with the permission of the persons involved. All other illustrations are composites of real situations, and any resemblance to people living or dead is coincidental.

Unless otherwise identified, all Scripture quotations in this publication are taken from the HOLY BIBLE: NEW INTERNATIONAL VERSION® (NIV®). Copyright © 1973, 1978, 1984 by International Bible Society. Used by permission of Zondervan Publishing House. All rights reserved. Other versions used include: *THE MESSAGE* (MSG). Copyright © 1993, 1994, 1995, 1996, 2000, 2001, 2002. Used by permission of NavPress Publishing Group; the *Amplified New Testament* (AMP), © The Lockman Foundation 1954, 1958; and the *King James Version* (KJV).

Renfroe, Anita, 1962-
    A purse-driven Christmas : so, what did you get me? / Anita Renfroe.
      p. cm.
    ISBN 1-57683-898-6
    1. Christmas. 2. Materialism--Religious aspects--Christianity.
    3. Christian life.   I. Title.
    BV45.R465 2005
    263'.915--dc22
                                            2005018769

Printed in Canada

1 2 3 4 5 6 7 8 9 10 / 09 08 07 06 05

FOR A FREE CATALOG OF NAVPRESS BOOKS & BIBLE STUDIES,
CALL 1-800-366-7788 (USA) OR 1-416-499-4615 (CANADA)

table of contents
chair of contents
sofa of contents

official
disclaimer

O kay, I realize "So, what did you get me?" is not the *true* meaning of Christmas.

I know about the blessings of giving versus those of receiving. I know we need to fight the materialism, greed, and shallow nature of our instant-gratification-oriented society. I'm aware our culture is focused on acquisition and the amassing of stuff. The amount of money spent on advertising in the USA for the express purpose of creating a shopping "itch" that must be retail "scratched" is larger than the Gross National Product of many countries in the world.

I get it. I get that "getting" isn't a very spiritual theme for the season.

However, Christmas is a time of year that is rife with expectation. I expect there will be some special time spent with people who mean a great deal to me and I will receive many wonderful gifts (mostly spiritual intangibles) as a result of the season. And Christmas *is* a great time to work on being a gracious receiver.

And that is something we tend to be very, very bad at. (Dangling preposition—get over it. Worrying about the dangling preposition is precisely the sort of behavior that makes the Christmas season problematic for perfectionists.)

We have been socialized first to be embarrassed by receiving an unexpected gift (be it a thing or be it words) and then to hide our embarrassment over receiving anything lavish with a lame comment. It's practically a truism in the South that we will say *anything* to deflect a compliment or a gift. We are famous for such inane statements as:

"Really, you shouldn't have." (how judgmental)

"It's too much." (for what?)

"Why on earth did you do that?" (hmmm, I don't know, maybe . . . love?)

I believe Christmas is the season for learning the grace of receiving as well as for relishing the joys of giving. Jesus came as a gift, and the gospel of John says that "his own received him not" (John 1:11, KJV). How rude.

So I come to you with a book that may be a relief from the usual Christmas literary fare. I offer you a smorgasbord of observational humor, a smattering of my personal recollections, and a dash of good sense (I leave it up to you to decide which is which). I do not claim to be writing a holiday classic for the ages, but if I succeed in brightening your spirits, alleviating an ounce of expectational guilt, or helping you realize you are not the only one who feels like the world spins too fast between Thanksgiving and New Year's Day, my mission will be accomplished.

Merry Christmas, Gentle Reader.

what's in the bag?

P urses at any time of year are a reliable tip-off to a girl's personality (or as I like to call it, Purse-onality). I have always maintained you can tell a lot about a woman by what is swinging from her arm. It's a statement about who she is and what her current station in life demands of her. These receptacles of the stuff of life offer a snapshot of our sense of style and our daily necessities. At Christmas, a girl has a perfect excuse to go hog wild! In fact, Christmas purses can take you to a whole 'nother level on the Purse-onality Scale.

There are some women who will not even acknowledge the season by changing their handbag. Their idea of getting in the Christmas spirit is placing some red and white mints inside their purse. It isn't particularly that they are Scrooge-ish; they just don't see the need for holiday accessorizing. They are nothing if not practical. These are the women who do not rearrange their furniture "for fun." They shop from a laminated grocery list and are stable to the point of boredom. They need spontaneous friends or else they would miss the season altogether.

There are other chicks who will change to a season-appropriate color of bag, but it won't have any adornment that announces the holidays. They will drag out their red bag from storage (where it has been since Valentine's Day) but would never think of purchasing a purse they would use only five weeks out of the year. *What a waste!* These women believe in a modicum of celebration without overdoing it. These are the friends who will go to a theme park with you but won't scream on the roller coasters. They will keep their arms and legs inside the car at all times. They are the classic, the understated.

And then there are the Purse-a-holics, who have a purse for every season. They have purses appropriate for any theme, and they revel in the variety. If they have a bag for St. Patrick's Day and one for Arbor Day, of *course* they would have their three or four favorite holiday bags in heavy rotation for December. This is their Christmas gift to the world! These girls have an even greater assortment of Christmas-decorated sweater sets and accessories that light up and/or jingle. They are happiest when the season provides them an excuse to show their stuff, and Christmas is nothing if not their reason to bring out their collections. These are your party instigators, and your life is not complete unless your circle of friends includes one or two of these free spirits. These are the friends who wouldn't be able to come bail you out of jail because they would be in there with you.

I have always fallen to the middle ground in the Christmas Purse-onality Continuum — not because I wouldn't love to accessorize for the holidays, but I simply can't remember where I stored the stuff from eleven months ago. It may seem pathetic, but if you can find your seasonal stuff only every other year, it's like all new stuff again!

Regardless of which purse makes it out the door with me, I truly love the shopping opportunities of Christmastime because while I am out questing for great gifts for others, I sometimes find great stuff for me. It almost feels wrong, but then I take it home and make my husband wrap it and give it to me later. That way, I always get exactly what I wanted.

Speaking of gift wrapping, it just ain't what it used to be. Back when this country was great, God-fearin' people used to teach their young-uns how to wrap their gifts with neat squared-off corners and hidden tape. Now they just throw their gifts into festive bags, stuff a piece of tissue on top, and act like they've really done something there. We had a family ban on any bags under the tree last year (as it entices the snoopers among us to an easy snoop). All our kids were forced to use their geometry knowledge of right angles to try to fashion a wrapping style that would cover the box without any ends being rolled up. I am sorry to say that the girl-child of our family had the hardest time with it. We are thinking of lifting the ban for her this year and encouraging her to keep her presents in her room until Christmas Eve to thwart the snoopers.

One of my personal-best Christmas presents didn't come in the traditional wrapping. My daughter was born on December first: not close enough to Christmas to endanger her birthday/Christmas differentiation (is that a word?), but during the full season swing, as her birthday follows close on the heels of Thanksgiving. In fact, the year she was born, we had a big snowstorm on Thanksgiving, and there were people in our church congregation on standby with their four-wheel drives had she decided to come right after the pumpkin pie. But she had her own ideas about her birth date (and I do agree that the first of any month is easiest to remember), so when she was born, I wanted to incorporate something of Christmas into her name. We had planned on naming her Celeste Elyse (très French, mais oui?) but quickly changed it to Elyse Noelle in honor of her birth month. It flowed off the tongue nicely, and I thought it sounded elegant.

A few weeks later, we received a letter of congratulations from a longtime friend of ours (Dr. James Flanagan, president of Luther Rice Seminary), and he noted that our naming of the new baby was positively brilliant. He was sure that we had been so clever in our arranging of the name, as the linguistic roots of "Elyse" (happy) and "Noelle" (birthday) meant that we had named our little girl "Happy Birthday." We were forced to admit to him that we weren't quite that smart. Elyse was our early Christmas gift in 1989, wrapped in a blanket instead of a box or a bag.

More recently, I received a gift from my husband in a non-standard gift bag, but it didn't immediately have the effect he was hoping for. Speaking from personal experience, I suggest that if you are presenting to someone a piece of jewelry that contains authentic gemstones, you leave it in some form of original packaging so that the recipient realizes the worth of the gift. John had bought me a beautiful inlaid onyx-and-diamond pinky ring.

He thought it would be a great idea to take it out of the Official Jeweler's Gift Box and slide it into a cute fabric pouch that they give you when you purchase jewelry at Chico's, a store better known for travel wear than for expensive jewelry (so that he could more easily disguise the gift by sticking it in the toe of my stocking sans box). When I came across the ring in the fabric pouch in my stocking, I assumed that this was a costume ring he got at Chico's (fair assumption, right ladies?). He was truly wounded that I didn't react more excitedly about the ring. It wasn't until about an hour later when I said, "Which Chico's did you find the ring at?" that he finally understood my understated response. When he explained that it was for real, he got a much bigger hug. Note to males: Keep it in the original box.

The little jewelry bags can be tricky enough, but the bags they load you up with at the mall these days are another deal entirely. They get larger every year, and they are unwieldy. We could even think of it as a physical fitness test of the season: The Toting Event.

Now, this challenge requires a good deal of training to build up much finger-joint stamina. Some serious shoppers start their fall regimen by loading up many full plastic grocery bags on a single finger and carrying them from the car to the kitchen from September through October so they will be in shape when Christmas push comes to shove. The pain one endures while the bags with uncomfortable handles mount on one's individual fingers is excruciating. I have heard that some regimes use this Heavy Shopping Bag with Uncomfortable Handles as a method of breaking down resistance in prisoners of war.

When you start off with one or two bags, you feel confident that you can continue shopping for another several hours. As you continue to add bags, however, a strange physics phenomenon occurs: The bags tend to weigh more and more as they settle in next to each other and swing from your crooked fingers. Because your fingers were never meant to have quite this much weight resting in their curled position, after the sixth bag is added to the mix, your finger joints will start to let you know that you should go out to your vehicle immediately and relieve this pain before forging ahead with any more buying and toting.

This is one excellent argument in favor of marriage. Husbands are so handy to have around for The Toting Event. Really. In fact, they welcome the excuse to exit the shopping center, as the mall air is kryptonite to the average male. Since men go to the mall so intermittently, they forget in between trips how debilitating its air can be. Your husband may agree to accompany you to the mall (it's only fair since you are risking your life in choosing the gifts for his mother and sisters), but once he enters, he starts feeling the power drain out of him little by little until he staggers to a bench with these words: "I'll just sit here until you're through." His manliness and pride will not allow him to admit to you that he is mere seconds from death, but if you're perceptive, you can actually see his skin turn strange colors. So you must periodically wave a TCBY cone under his nose and let him go to the car if you want him to live to tote another day.

As the holiday season draws nigh, may I encourage you, my

dear Fellow Toters, to sling on the most festive bag you can get away with and let your Christmas Purse-onality shine. Remember to take an extra measure of patience and joy with you wherever you go. And be careful not to miss the most precious of gifts that sometimes arrive in unusual packaging.

Carry on!

yule log

There's an old Elvis Presley Christmas song that goes like this: "Oh why can't every day be like Christmas?" I mean, it's a beautiful song, but the answer to the question seems quite obvious to me. Why can't every day be like Christmas? I'll tell you why: because we could never bear it. If every day *were* like Christmas, we would be bleary-eyed from late-night toy assemblies, neurotic and overwrought from biting our tongues around our visiting relatives, jittery about the impending credit card statements, bloated from all the sweets at the requisite parties, and worried about our children's ability to survive their prosperity.

This is supposed to be "the most wonderful time of the year," and in many ways, it is. There is a certain pervasive goodwill that is extended to friends and strangers alike—unless, that is, they are vying for the last parking spot near the front of the mall.

There is at least one category of people who do not participate in the Last Space in the Parking Lot Quest (because all their shopping is already done, don't you know?). Let's give props to all the Organized Christmas People (aka The OCPs). These are the ones whose obsessive-compulsive tendencies become an advantage rather than a disorder and the rest of us would hope for even half their organizational skill. OCPs have Christmas savings accounts with automatic monthly deposits deducted painlessly from their paycheck so that they awaken on October first to find that their Christmas fund is loaded and ready to fire. If they are true OCPs, though, their shopping is fully completed during the Labor Day Weekend Sales and their gifts are wrapped and stacked long before October first, so the money is just a bonus.

These people also have lists (and by this I mean "small accounting ledgers," aka The Yule Log) filed by year as to who they sent Christmas cards to, what they have purchased for people, each person's sizes and color preference, each person's reaction to the present, files for the receipts, and potential gifts ideas for upcoming years. They see the Christmas season as a chance to show off their high-achiever ranking. It is their Organizational World Championship, so to speak.

I have a friend who is like this. I had to ask her about her list of categories since I would have no idea where to even begin to make such a Yule Log. But for people like Stacy, this is just a normal part of her season — just like looking high and low for receipts is a normal part of my season. For people like me who fit neatly into the category of non-planner FBSPs (Fly By the Seat of Pants), Christmas is a slightly more muddled experience.

All of the organizational experts seem to agree that the best way to bring order to the chaos that can accompany the holidays is summed up in a single word: simplify. They close their eyes when they say it, as if to convey the utter peace that will sweep over your life if you can just pare things down to the essentials. (Notice, however, that the people urging you to "simplify" are also the ones who want you to buy their complex product lines of books and videos and planners.)

Still, our family thought these organizational experts might be on to something, so we started our own crusade to simplify the season. Our first decision was to ditch the whole Christmas card thing altogether. Our rationale is that those truly close to us would be receiving a Christmas present from us in the mail or we'd be seeing them over the holidays (thus, no "greeting" card necessary). This leaves a great number of people in the "We Haven't Contacted You All Year Because There's Really No Reason To" category. We figured these people probably wouldn't want to get a Christmas card from us, as it would only serve to remind them that we didn't like them enough to keep in touch, thus reopening the social wound, so to speak. We thought, *Why make it worse?* So, we have the two categories: Those Who Don't Need a Card Because They Know We Love Them versus Those Who Probably Don't Need a Card to Remind Them How We Haven't Cared Enough to Contact Them All Year Long. Simple enough, right? Thus we dispensed with the Christmas cards.

This, however, does not stop us from *receiving* Christmas cards. And we love that because we know we must fall into one of those categories with all the people who send them to us! It's fun to try to decide which you are. I have started trying to respond with a personal letter in January to all the people who personally *signed* their cards (not had them imprinted). I think that people who have their cards imprinted are the laziest of the lazy. It's okay if the card is from your dentist's office, but highly impersonal if you are Joe Q. Friend. This makes us card snobs, but one has to uphold standards in one's life.

We also receive quite a few of the Christmas newsletters. Oh, joy. We have a few friends who make theirs a poem with a very consistent rhyme scheme. I don't think I could make my year's events rhyme—like, what rhymes with catheter? We have other friends who make their newsletters a pictorial year in review. I think they Photoshop themselves into various exotic climes (can they really be vacationing that much?). The one I wait for every Christmas is from a family with whom we maintain annual contact. The wife writes a *very long* newsletter, in third person (as if we didn't know that she is writing it), about how amazing and brilliant and beautiful her children are (they may be) and how fabulous their family life is (it might be) and how spiritual her life is (hours of Bible study daily), blah, blah, blah. I'm sure you get these, too. Don't they make you feel like sticking your finger back near your tonsils for some relief?

If reality TV shows are so popular, why can't we have reality Christmas newsletters? Just once I'd like to receive one that says, "We've had a mixed bag this year: lots of life lessons, some ups and downs with our kids, a few setbacks financially. My husband's hair transplant wasn't the success we were hoping for, but it looks pretty good over the top of one ear. So, how are you?"

Another effort to simplify our holidays has actually made it more complicated. We had a semi-brilliant idea a few years back that we would find one really great gift, buy it in multiples, and give it to just about everyone on our list. As I said, it seemed like a great idea, but sometimes we have a few left over, which we save in bins in the attic. The problem is, when Christmas comes 'round again, we can't remember if people were on the list last year, or if they've become better friends in the interim and thus should receive this year the great thing from last year. It's maddening. So, if we meet you somewhere this year, remind us that you are a "newer friend," because we've got a lot of great gifts in the attic that are just waiting for a whole new batch of lucky recipients.

Unlike us FBSP shoppers, the OCPs are ultracool, ultimately confident, and way out of my league. These people order their gifts via the Internet, shipped straight to the door of their loved one, perfectly packed and impeccably wrapped. They did not break a sweat emotionally or physically questing for an appropriate gift. They put on their pajamas, brewed a cup of chai, and clicked their way to Christmas Gift Easy Street. If they were out amongst the riffraff on Christmas Eve, it was merely to take in the sights and sounds and thank the Lord that they were not like the rest of us. (Christmas Pharisees.) If you are one of these people, please try to curb your feelings of superiority.

The rest of us view the Christmas-shopping experience as an emotional and physical decathlon of sorts. And it would not be so bad if the Parking Lot Stalk-a-Spot Race were not on the docket. But it is. If you do not excel in this event, you are gonna be one miserable pup.

Parking lots at Christmastime are not the place to view peace on earth or peace of mind. They are more like "piece of my mind." It brings out the predator in us all, as it is a study in supply and demand. There are a limited number of spaces and more-than-usual occupants. We actually stalk the people walking out to their cars. (Don't act like you don't do it. You know you do.) We see them crossing in front of the store, headed for their car, and we turn up the row with them and go v-e-r-y s-l-o-w-l-y so as not to tip them off that we are stalking them. If they turn around to look at us, we look the other way. This stealth operation goes on until they either cut across to another row (how dare they?) or arrive at their car only to open the trunk, deposit some bags from The Toting Event, and wave us off as they mouth the words, "I'm not leaving."

Coises. Foiled again. We are doomed to continue circling the parking lot like a buzzard for another thirty minutes, waiting for the next person to stalk. I believe that all the Faux Leave-ers should identify themselves as such before they get to their car. Can't we get some legislation for that?

Once a space does open up (for a nanosecond), it becomes a struggle for supremacy between The Quicker (small turn radius, thin body) versus The Bigger (SUVs and all other vehicles with names that evoke testosterone). The smaller cars have the advantage in the agility department, but the large bodies can intimidate merely by the fact they can squish a Toyota like a soda can. And if you have a Hummer, I suppose you park the way an elephant sits: anywhere you want to. Personally, I've always wanted to ask Hummer owners this question: "If your vehicle is meant to drive in all terrains and take all kinds of abuse, why do you slow down for speed bumps?"

As much as I admire the OCPs, my FBSP ways are possibly too ingrained to be rehabilitated. If I find a preprinted Yule Log with an interactive chip that automatically registers every purchase, files every receipt, and logs each recipient response, I might see my way clear to better Christmas organization and an earlier finish to my shopping list. Until then, I'll be the one stalking you in the parking lot.

so i married santa claus

T here are a lot of subliminal things that go into choosing our life partner. Scientists tell us that sometimes women will choose a husband based on facial proportions and symmetrical features. Other researchers contend that we choose based on certain scents that are difficult to identify but are strongly tied to our childhoods. Some women choose a man based on how much he reminds her of her father. I think I married John because he is the closest thing I could get to Santa Claus.

Now, I'm not saying that he's fat and jolly—quite the opposite. He is a lean, not-mean love machine. I'm just saying that he loves Christmas with childlike abandon and isn't ashamed to exhibit his love of the season. Plus, he sometimes smells like sugar cookies. (I buy his soap.)

Though John's vocational choice was to be in church ministry for all of his adult life, he definitely has a second calling in Display/Décor. It's interesting that the culture has recently created a category for men who are "straight but not afraid to exfoliate."

They call these guys *metrosexuals*. The definition implies that there are men who take care of their skin, can cook and decorate, yet are actually heterosexual. I believe that as more men are being liberated from what constitutes "manly" activities, this presents problems that women have not had to deal with in the past. Now the guys are borrowing our moisturizers, taking up our appointment availability at the spas, and venturing into hitherto "female only" arenas. I can't tell you how many times I've been to my nail place lately only to see a guy in the spa pedicure chair with his gnarly toes in the same water bath that I am scheduled to use next. I don't care *what* they clean out the basin with in between soaks—I am *not* sticking my feet in there.

My man not only falls into the metrosexual category but also has created his own niche within this new definition. He was raised in Mississippi and cannot deny his Rankin County roots, yet he has a great eye for décor, so I call him my "Redneck Metrosexual." For example, he loves to change out the monthly display on the front hall table to match the seasons, but he has no problem shooting squirrels off our back deck. (Perfectly harmless unless he shoots out his own eye or misses the squirrel and inadvertently hits the neighbor's dog.) We are the only people I know of who have a sleeve of BBs on the fireplace mantel and the BB gun behind the drapes next to the French doors so John can run out and shoot like Jed Clampett. This is a man who uses a hefty gas-powered chain saw to trim our front shrubs yet nimbly shapes them to look like perfect Hershey's Kisses.

My Redneck Metrosexual Man is the envy of all the neighborhood women. Last Halloween, I was at the door greeting the trick-or-treaters from our cul-de-sac. As some newer neighbors followed their little cutie pies to our door, one of the women commented that they all love it when we leave our front door open so they can view the table that changes every month and enjoy the beautiful decorations that signal the upcoming season. She said, "I don't know how you do it!" I just shook my head and said, "I don't, but I'll be happy to call my husband up here so you can tell him." I wish I had a Polaroid of her face. It was as if I had just told her that my husband was Martha Stewart. I'm sure he'll be invited to give a demonstration at the women's club any day now. And he would be well groomed for it, too.

When Christmas rolls around, John sees it as the Olympics of Decorating—not as in, "I will put up more lights and yard ornaments than anyone on my block," but more like, "My house will be the most elegantly decorated in my neighborhood." Because we spent seven years of our married life in Virginia, he devotes a great deal of time to putting together a Williamsburg-esque half-round of fruit that goes over our front door. It has magnolia leaves, oranges, lemons, apples, pears, and a pineapple in the middle (which is great if the weather stays cold, but if it warms up, we get drippy fruit sap on our heads whenever we leave the house). I am always tempted to eat the fruit he picks out for this project, which is probably why he doesn't let me help anymore. He also makes fresh pine swags that surround the front door and trains spotlights on them so they are accentuated just so. There are only white lights adorning his Hershey's Kiss shrubs, and he nestles spotlighted carolers near the walkway, hangs matching wreathes outside every window, and puts Williamsburg lights in each window sill. This consumes an entire Saturday, and that's before he starts inside the house.

When his attention turns indoors, no surface (flat or otherwise) is safe. He decorates everything—and he does it well. There is Christmas paraphernalia everywhere you look. It's a wonderful thing.

And his Christmas enthusiasm extends to his ability to make the Christmas season last from Thanksgiving Saturday until the kids go back to school in January. He also presents each of us with The Twelve Days of Christmas presents (not the actual calling birds and French hens, but a present for each of the days leading up to Christmas Day). I remember one of John's friends asking him to consider backing off on the pre-Christmas gift giving, as the friend's wife was asking him why *he* didn't give *her* a dozen gifts!

I am thankful to have a man who truly enjoys all that the season brings and has given our kids a great launching pad for their own traditions as they start their families in the future.

I have a button that reads, "I strive to live every day as if it were my birthday." That's how John feels about Christmas.

orna-
mental

The quest for The Perfect Christmas Tree—it's a seasonal ordeal. For some, it involves a trip to the local Christmas tree farm to see them growing live, judge them like they're modeling for a Miss Christmas Tree pageant, take a handsaw to the base of the favored tree and cut it down in the prime of its life, and bring it home caveman style. For others, the quest involves visiting the local roadside stands where the trees have been carted in from nether regions and choosing from a lovely selection of various pines and evergreens. At this point, you must decide if you will choose to support the local Boy Scout troop and pay twenty bucks extra, or go down to Home Depot and live with your Scrooge-ishness.

There are many others who choose to forego the yearly tree-choice-trauma, as they have chosen to go artificial and never have to wrestle with the tree stand, deal with dropping needles, or remember to water. They also have the option of leaving their tree lights on from year to year, but this can backfire when one light goes out and there's no clue as to where the single offender is located. We have actually resorted to scissors to get those tightly wound light strings off an artificial tree. It's slight overkill, but getting them off any other way takes too much time.

Do you remember when strings of lights cost a lot of money? About ten years ago, they went from $12 a box down to $2.99. That's one price drop that will eventually add a few years to our lives. I believe that was the exact time we decided that it was *not* worth it to sit around on the floor for an hour with a bulb tester, trying to find the one bulb that was out.

Pinning down the genesis of tree decorating is a little slippery, but most scholars point to Germany as the country of origin. It seems that the evergreen coming indoors was (at first) a pagan ritual to bring the only green thing in the dead of winter indoors to celebrate life. It seems that Christians appropriated the ritual for themselves around the time of Martin Luther, as he added lights and some other decorations. (What a feather in his cap: discovering grace *and* decorating the Christmas tree.)

When we were newlyweds, John and I lived in housing for married college students. These duplexes might as well have had a sign hanging outside that read, "If you are harebrained enough to believe you can hold down three part-time jobs, cram for exams, *and* nurture a marriage, the least we can do is give you low-cost shelter with gas heat that may or may not asphyxiate you." We worked on our little duplex for a few weeks before we got married (between semesters) and made our little love nest as cozy as a forty-year-old half-a-house could be. I recently drove down that street and saw that the college had bulldozed our duplexes and sold the property for frontage for a superstore. And we had worked so hard on that vinyl floor . . .

Our very first Christmas tree was truly a Charlie Brown Christmas Special. I don't mean *the* Charlie Brown Christmas Special (the one on TV with the great Vince Guaraldi Skating Song and the children singing "Christmas time is here . . ."); I mean the Charlie Brown Christmas *tree* (the last one left on the lot with very little in the pine needle department). It smelled great but had about eighteen inches between branches. That sounds sad, but it really worked well, as we had practically nothing but a string of lights and a few "Our First Christmas Together 1982" ornaments to hang on it. Trimming the tree back then was blissfully uncomplicated. We had no idea we were being historically accurate, as this sort of tree was *preferred* in the 1600s in Germany because the only lights they had on their trees were decidedly not electric, and who wants to have an indoor bonfire for Christmas?

With the birth of each of our children came the accompanying ornaments celebrating their entrance into the world, as well as all the ornaments they crafted for us with their widdle hands. Some were cute, some were, well, definitely original. The cute ones were hung in conspicuous places on the tree (which took up slightly more space each year than did our original Charlie Brown Christmas Special). The less-cute ones had their own place of honor: The Backside of the Tree. We used to tell the kids that we put these ornaments on the window side for everyone to see as they passed by the house. Cruel, I know.

Hallmark stores came up with a great marketing idea of

ornaments with the year inscribed on them. We used to buy them for half price after the holidays because we liked the way they looked, never projecting that this would be a problem. We have one with "Baby's First Christmas 1987"—only problem being that we didn't *have* a baby that particular year. Our kids were very confused and thought we had hidden their other sibling from them. I'll have to get a Sharpie and fix that.

Handmade ornaments are coveted items in some circles. I have friends who go to parties where the only entertainment is that the participants exchange ornaments they have made with their very own hands. This is risky unless you are selective in your guest list. There are women who are able to follow the instructions and those who are not. The ones who are craft-challenged always look for something that is fail-safe. These lesser crafters will default to projects that require only plastic canvas and yarn. My friend's mother-in-law discovered she could pull off this particular craft and has, to date, given her daughter-in-law more than two hundred items made out of it. In order to remain in the good family graces, my friend displays the entire collection every single year.

Even if you are the Queen of Crafts and have had a magazine and television show celebrating your craft prowess, you can have an off day. I read on my Web news page that the formerly incarcerated domestic diva Martha Stewart participated in the Christmas-decorating contest at her prison. She and her fellow elves didn't have an actual tree to decorate (prison rules don't permit them, as they could be fashioned into battering rams), but they didn't want to miss out on being orna-mental, even behind bars. Each group of prisoners was given twenty-five dollars worth of glitter, ribbons, construction paper, and glue. Martha instructed her cellmates to make origami cranes. (Can't you just hear her now? "Jody—no, no, no. You fold the upper corner down toward your leg irons and the right corner toward your tattoo.") And then they hung them across the ceiling and in front of the (barred) window. What could she have been thinking? As if the judges wouldn't infer a reference to "jailbirds"? Martha's group suffered an embarrassing defeat. Awww. That must have been a little hard to swallow for Miss It's-a-Good-Thing. It just goes to show that you can think you're All That with an unlimited budget and thirty-five production assistants, but if you're working with what's on hand and have inmates to fold your paper birds, consider yourself equalized, dearie.

We can't find any guidance from the official etiquette dames regarding the question of the right time to *remove* the Christmas decorations. When is the optimum time to take them down? I have seen (only in movies) that there are some people who don't even put their trees up until Christmas Eve. Who *are* these people? Don't they know that part of the joy of having a tree is its being up at least a couple of weeks prior so they can enjoy the lights and watch the presents and pine needles stack up around the bottom?

These are the same people who take the tree down the day after Christmas. They obviously don't do quite as much decorating as we do, because if we waited until Christmas to do all that we do and then took it down immediately afterward, we would miss Christmas altogether. I believe that these people are secretly Christmas haters and just want to have the least amount of Christmas environment allowable by law. Their mantra is, "It's not Christmas yet, not yet, not yet, not yet—now it is—great, it's over already—get the stuff outta here!" We leave our tree lights on twenty-four hours a day from the time the tree goes up, and we don't even care if our electricity bill spikes for several weeks. Some things are just worth it.

Our penchant as Southerners for leaving the Christmas lights up on our houses all year long is so cliché that our fellow Georgians actually use it as a measure of redneck-ness. If you don't leave your lights up, you're not in the club. And I understand the rationale. If you risk life and limb to string them up there, it seems only smart to just leave them up there. The older I get, the closer together Christmases seem to be. It feels like we just got the decorations put away and then it's time to get them back out again. Some people describe it à la the Quantum Toilet-Paper-Roll Theorem: The less toilet paper left on the roll, the faster it goes. But it's not the lights attached to the rooftops that really make you a redneck—it's the plastic Santa, Frosty, and Rudolph on the front lawn that seem a little out of place when you have to mow around them in July.

Our family has now reached the stage in our tree-trimming evolution where a single tree will not accommodate all the ornaments we have made/collected/been given/bought at the after-Christmas sales. We now have the following trees in different rooms of our house:

- *The Family Tree* in the living room—A real, live tree with sentimental ornaments.

- *The Gingerbread Tree* in the kitchen—Small and spindly, artificial, with food-related ornaments such as dried orange slices and, I swear this is true, dried okra pods with Santa faces painted on them. (If you need me to send a digital photo to prove it, I will.)
- *The Music/Victorian/White House Official Yearly Ornament Tree* in the dining room—Artificial pencil tree that fits neatly in any corner or window without taking up extra room space. We decorate this one with many pretty things that do not disturb our digestion.
- *The Snowman Stuff Got to Be Too Much for the Entryway Table Tree* in the front hall—Another artificial tree purely for passersby to enjoy.

I am aware that our multiple-tree scenario is not reminiscent of our early uncomplicated Christmases, but all these trees represent our family's growth and our desire to bring attention to the season of celebration in every room of our home. We dig that each tree focuses on different aspects of Christmas. Besides, you can't let the ornaments commingle or intermarry. They will be confused.

a wonder-
full life

I have a very clear recollection of where I was the first time I saw the movie *It's a Wonderful Life*. I was in my grandmother's hospital room in my hometown over my first college holiday break. Nana was in the last stages of breast cancer and was experiencing some hallucinations due to the medications she was being given for her pain. Believing that someone was trying to shoot her, she would occasionally get up out of bed and crouch down behind it. Someone needed to stay in the room with her to keep her from getting out of the bed and trying to leave the hospital. (Even in her weakened state, Nana was one powerfully determined woman.)

I was glad to stay with her, as Nana had been a big part of my life. My mom and I lived with her and my granddad from the time I was two years old to the age of ten. I would hang out with Nana while my mother was at work, and Nana spoiled me rotten. Her broiler-made cheese toast was my favorite snack, and her garlic dill pickles will never be rivaled. She would watch her "stories" in the afternoon (*As the World Turns* and *Guiding Light*) while she did her sewing. It was the only time I recall seeing my grandmother sitting down. I would pretend to be napping, but I enjoyed watching her "stories," too. Not a bad life for a kid.

But Nana also had a mind to encourage God's gifts in my life and always told me I could do whatever God put in my heart to do. I believed her. So when it became apparent that the cancer was not going to be beaten back, my holiday vacation plans were set, and I packed my bags to stay on watch with my nana for as long as my college break lasted.

Very late one night, I turned the television away from the bed so that the light wouldn't bother Nana, and I proceeded to flip around between the channels (three networks and one public broadcasting station—not like the overwhelming number of choices we have today). When I came across a black-and-white movie starring Jimmy Stewart and Donna Reed, it wasn't so far along in the story line that I couldn't pick up the plot. I was instantly drawn into the drama. I'm not sure if it was because of my sense that life was fragile, due to Nana's illness, or because I was just old enough now to get the importance of the message of the movie, but I knew that the sentiment was exactly right: that every life matters and no one is poor if he has friends. I remember crying as the townspeople of Bedford Falls came to George Bailey's rescue and the angel, Clarence, declared, "Each man's life touches so many other lives. If he wasn't around, it would leave an awful hole." It was a wonderful, emotional night for me.

The next Christmas was our family's first without Nana, but

watching that movie again on TV brought warm memories of my precious last days with her. A couple years later, John and I were newlyweds, still in college with a Charlie Brown Christmas tree in our little duplex apartment, and we spent much of Christmas at our parents' houses, where we watched the movie yet again. By now it was entering the category of Family Holiday Tradition.

The first Christmas John and I spent in our first house—in Star, Mississippi (a parsonage)—we gave each other "wish" presents. These are items you can't afford but "wish" you had enough money to give to someone. I cut out a picture from a catalog of a VCR (they were very expensive in 1983) and glued it into a card with a poem about how I would give the coveted item to John if I could. He, in turn, gave me a VHS tape of *It's a Wonderful Life*, even though we had no VCR to play it in.

Ironic in the most O. Henry-ish sense.

I became an *It's a Wonderful Life* trivia buff and found out the reason for its popularity with TV station programmers. Apparently, the owners of the 1946 copyright somehow overlooked the fact that their license needed to be renewed, so it lapsed in 1974. Television networks could now air the movie without paying royalties, and the result was that the classic was broadcast over and over again during the Christmas season. The message of the movie resonated with the masses. It was a fitting contribution to the world for a script that originally bore the title of *The Greatest Gift*.

John and I became so enamored with this movie that we began over the course of the next few years to have "IAWL" theme parties. You have to think the interactive *Rocky Horror Picture Show* phenomenon of the mid-seventies, where people would dress up like the characters and bring props for the different scenes and throw things at the screen, booing or cheering depending on the character. For our annual IAWL Party, we would issue the invitation with a list of suggested props to bring. These would include Monopoly money for when there was a run on the bank, kazoos to hum "God Bless America" during George's speeches to Mr. Potter, flags to wave while we hummed, a bell to ring so angels could get their wings, rice to throw when George and Mary got married, fake snow to throw whenever it snowed, umbrellas to put up whenever it rained, robes to don during the post-pool episode, and tinsel to put in our hair like Zu Zu had in hers during the last scene. We would get up and dance our pitiful Charlestons during the dance contest and hiss and throw paper balls each time Mr. Potter came on the screen. The parties got so big that we finally had to move them to the church, where we could project the movie onto something bigger.

It seems everyone loves this movie for his or her own reasons, but I think it speaks especially lovingly to the disappointed and brokenhearted souls. Psychologists and researchers tell us that the holidays tend to bring out feelings of despondency and hopelessness in people, like what George Bailey experienced in the movie. As I am not a theologian, I won't comment on the accuracy of Clarence coming back to earth to have a chance to win back his wings. Nowhere in the Bible do we find anything that tells us that humans ever become angels (in fact, Scripture claims that mankind is "a little lower than the angels" [Psalm 8:5, KJV] in the hierarchy of creation). But I do know that the messages of *It's a Wonderful Life* are rich:

- Your life is of infinite worth and impacts many others, regardless of your recognition of that fact.
- The world would be a different (and worse!) place had you never been born.
- We make our choices, our choices make us, and the dreams that get derailed along the way only make for a life filled with another form of sweetness.
- You can do everything as uprightly as you know how, and unfair things may still happen to you.
- No matter how desperate you are, God will hear your cry for help.
- God works things out in unimaginable ways.

Though we cannot always see our angels as George saw Clarence, they are with us. Though we will never hear the symphony of prayers arising on our behalf as in the opening scene of this movie, people are standing in the gap for us, even when we least sense it.

My prayer for you is that you would know there is always hope, even in the darkest of circumstances—and that every life (yes, your life) is wonder-full, indeed.

the poinsettia executioner

Let us turn our attention for a moment to the less attractive aspects of our Christmas rituals. There is, indeed, a Dark Side to the season, the elements no one really wants to discuss openly. This includes the waste. There are the batteries, which give of their stored energy and are then tossed aside for new ones. The number of bows that are sitting atop beautifully wrapped packages one day and in the bottom of the Hefty trash bag the next is staggering. The live pines that decorate our homes at least have a second life, as they are sent to the chippers to become our spring mulch. But today I would like to discuss another form of this senseless waste that hits home for our family: the lowly poinsettia.

I've already established that my man loves Christmas. But in the area of Poinsettia Excess, John is one tortured soul. He feels that a houseful of poinsettias is a necessity of the season but then is tormented by weeks and weeks of sorrow as they all eventually lose their will to live. It is as if they know they aren't in Mexico anymore. And you can't fool them by playing Spanish TV, either.

I believe I know how his poinsettia obsession all got started. John has been an associate pastor for most of our married life. In our church, we had some Christmas traditions that necessitated the purchase of poinsettias by the truckload. For a few years, we had a choral presentation called "The Living Christmas Tree," which consisted of a tall wooden platform with several rows on which singers would stand. As it got taller, the number of people in each row decreased until you got to the top and there was room for just one. (We always had a skinny, wiry singer at the top of the tree, just as you choose someone small for the top of a cheerleader pyramid.) We needed some foliage to cover up the wooden edifice, and for "The Living Christmas Tree," about two hundred pots of poinsettias sufficed superbly.

We also had a church tradition of offering poinsettias for sale each Christmas in honor of the memory of a loved one. These were nice-sized plants wrapped in the cool gold-and-red foil that covered the plastic pots. Church members would purchase them in bulk (they were very reasonable since we received a significant discount for the volume order), and the plants would remain as decoration for the stage area up until the Christmas Eve service, at which time anyone who donated monies for the poinsettias was welcome to take the flowers home.

Because many of our church members left to visit relatives out of state before Christmas Eve, there were always a bunch of orphaned poinsettias to deal with. The church offices would be closed for the week, and it fell to my husband (as he was the associate pastor—aka The Minister of Everything Else or The Minister

Who Actually Does All the Work) to find a home for them. And he tried valiantly to place as many orphaned poinsettias as possible in good, loving homes. We took as many as we could to shut-ins and nursing homes, but we always had many left over. John couldn't bring himself to let them die alone at the church, so he would bring them home with him. (I am just thankful he doesn't feel the same way about stray cats.)

There were poinsettias everywhere — lining our staircase, on the fireplace hearth, on top of the refrigerator, in the windowsills, on top of the TV, on the nightstands by our bed, in the bathroom! If there was an open spot, we plugged a pot into it. And when the plants were happy, John was happy.

This bliss lasted about ten days. But as the calendar pages turned to mid-January, our little plants felt that their days of usefulness were past and began to drop leaves daily. I do not exaggerate when I tell you my husband would spend the next eight to ten weeks trying to keep all those plants alive. He would water them, mist them, pick off the wilting leaves, talk to them — *anything* to keep them from dying on his watch.

You may be the sort of person who tosses your poinsettias in the trash three days after Christmas and never looks back. Not my John. So the Poinsettia Death Watch would commence. It would start with the ones near the fireplace; they were the first to drop their leaves due to their proximity to heat. Truth be told, they were the lucky ones. Their demise was quick. The others were not so fortunate.

Some poinsettias are apparently genetically stronger than

others: They just don't know when to give up. These determined little fighters would hold on to their colored leaves even when all of their green leaves had dropped away. They were no longer lush Christmas décor but spindly reminders that Valentine's Day could not be more than a week away. John would become sadder and sadder as he became unable to nurse the poinsettias back to their former glory, so he spent his time moving the pathetic things around the house to less conspicuous spots. It was too early to transplant them, and besides, we were nowhere near their native Mexican climate. I tried to offer comfort by reminding John they were only seasonal flora and had a full and happy life, as flowers go. But he could not bring himself to chuck them.

So it fell to me to be the Poinsettia Executioner. There would always come a day in February when I would take the foil wrappers off the pots and tote them out to the compost pile to return the flowers to the earth from whence they came. It's the least a compassionate soul could do.

In the last few years, John has weaned himself from the Houseful of Poinsettias mindset and become relatively content with a number somewhere around a dozen. Sure, it's less to look at, but for him it's also less to grieve over. However, if you happen to see a tall, handsome man with a grocery cart full of poinsettias when the store marks them down on Christmas Eve, it's probably my man.

seasonal guilt complex

It is my (humble but nonetheless right) opinion that it all started with those pins and cards that said, "Jesus is the reason for the season." We've all seen that little phrase imprinted on pens, stationery, plates, bumper stickers, magnets, and many a changeable church sign. It's catchy. It rhymes. It sums up the bottom line of Christmas. It has also laid a new layer of guilt over the Christmas experience.

Back in the day, I used to present a mini-seminar for women's groups that I cleverly titled "How to Keep Christ in Christmas." In this little talk, I had brilliant ideas, such as different Advent activities to do with your kids and lots of tips to ensure that your children would understand the true meaning of Christmas and not turn out to be card-carrying atheists. In my research of innovative ways to add meaning to seasonal activities, I came up with several gems, including placing preprinted tags on every candy cane with the story of how the candy cane represented redemption and using cookie cutters for our sugar cookies that were only in religiously symbolic shapes. A friend of mine had a tradition of putting up the manger scene without the baby Jesus in it and starting off the season with him in a far region of the house, moving Him closer to the manger every day as the calendar moved closer to Christmas Day. For the life of me, I can't remember why that seemed like such a good idea, but it was one of the ones I strongly advocated in my little seminar. I realized only much later that if you couldn't remember where you left the baby Jesus doll from one day to the next, or the dog found him and carried him off, that could be problematic.

I became an amateur Christmas symbolist, researching the meanings behind everything we did and reveling in the Christmas trivia and minutia. I would also talk for a good thirty minutes about our responsibility as Christians to choose only the sorts of ornaments that would help our friends and family understand Christ and how it was so important to keep the focus laser sharp for the Christmas season. The very earnest women in these seminars would listen with rapt attention and take detailed notes while I gave them even *more* things to do during the already insanely busy time of year to ensure that their families did not get the wrong idea as to what the season was really all about.

When I think of this now, I just want to go back in time and tell myself to shut up.

In the ensuing years, I came to realize the already-obvious truth about Christmas: Apart from Christ, it's not "Christmas" — it's just "-mas." I've observed that many of us who profess to live for Christ 24/7/365 feel a need to overly "represent" during the holiday season. Whence the pressure? I would like to stake my claim here and say that we don't have to worry that no one will understand Christmas unless we continually reexplain it. The apostle Peter tells us to be ready to give an answer for the hope that is within us (see 1 Peter 3:15). This presumes that someone is *asking* about the hope we possess. It's much better when someone asks about your faith; it means they actually want to know and are ready to listen because of some quality that emanates from Christ living in you, not because you decorated with the most overtly "Christian" of ornaments.

Who on earth decided to embrace this pile of expectations and add yet another opportunity to feel like abject spiritual failures if we don't imbue every moment with meaning? Can I just peel the monkey off your back for a moment? I find it hard to believe that Jesus is seated at the right hand of the Father getting all bothered that we aren't meeting some unwritten standard of properly celebrating the season. Note: It *is* spiritual by virtue of whose birth it is we are celebrating.

If you want to express your love for your family with extravagant gifts and you can afford to do so, then by all means lavish them as the Father lavished us with the gift of His son and as the wise men brought extravagant gifts from afar. If you want to feast with your friends and family to celebrate the gift that they are in your life, go for it! If your heart of compassion compels you to take up your proverbial towel and serve, then go forth to the homeless shelter, serve dinner, and distribute gifts of clothing and blankets. Should you choose to purchase no presents and give your money to fund an endeavor that engages your passion, give with all your heart! If you want to invite your neighbors over and extend to them the gift of hospitality, do so with gusto! If you want to bake cookies with your children and smear icing all over your noses and laugh until you cry, do it—and don't worry that your activities are not "spiritual" enough. That kind of thinking only kills the very joy and freedom that Christ came to give us.

If Christ lives in you 365 days a year, you don't have to be any more "Christian" during the Christmas season. In fact, it's impossible to pull off.

He is the reason for the season, but the season may be slightly off. We know that December probably isn't the time of year when Christ was actually born (the scholars think it was closer to springtime); it's just the time that we have chosen to honor the fact that he was born—or as the *The Message* Bible puts it, "The Word became flesh and blood, and moved into the neighborhood" (John 1:14). Jesus became helpless to help us when we couldn't help ourselves. So take it for what it is: a great reason to celebrate!

And might I remind you of the fact that the first Christmas was as messy as any we've experienced in our own day? This fact inspires us to remember the significance of that first Christmas, right in the middle of our holiday strangeness.

When you are persevering through the travel madness that accompanies the oft insane desire to be with relatives in your hometown, think of Mary and Joseph making the long journey back to their ancestral home for the government-imposed census.

When your hotel reservations get lost in cyberspace, think of Mary and Joseph looking for a room and getting a barn instead.

When you are fighting the crowds at the mall, think of how the population must have swelled in Bethlehem after Jesus' birth.

When you are untangling the tenth string of lights, think of the star that guided the wise men to the manger.

When you are loaded down with boxes and bags and it seems like a mile to your parking space, think of how far the wise men had to carry *their* gifts.

Perhaps all the weirdness of the season is, in fact, a great reminder of what a mess the first Christmas was. And look how well it turned out.

the snowman chronicles

On our Famous Front Table, which sports all manner of seasonal fare year-round, sits an odd assortment of snowmen and snow paraphernalia during the winter months. There's an old-timey box of fake snowflakes, a few snow globes, and many forms of the classic snowman shape. We are snow lovers who live in a region that doesn't get much.

Here in Atlanta, we have several different sorts of TV weather people to choose from. There are the pretty boys who are only reading the teleprompter (you can't trust them because just last week you saw them acting similarly authoritative while reading the sports from another teleprompter—we know they are there only because they have good hair); there are the women who may be bona fide meteorologists but don't want to seem like Miss Know-It-All, so they settle for Miss Congeniality (I think they should be more proud of their brains); and there are the not-so-great-looking old men with bad hairpieces. Personally, I trust the old guys. Why would they lie? If they haven't lost their jobs due to their age or looks, they must be telling the truth about the weather. Besides, if they are making their predictions based on the projected storm paths *and* their aging joints, they are possibly way more accurate than Mister Pretty Weatherboy.

If the weather forecaster on any of the Atlanta affiliates happens to mention a chance of snow (no matter how small), I run to the snowman table, light a few candles, and hope fervently for those flakes to materialize. I stock up on hot chocolate and gingerbread cake ingredients (they are plentiful, as most people are stocking up on toilet paper, batteries, bread, and milk—how unimaginative of them). We have a family pact that whenever it snows, I make a gingerbread cake. Needless to say, we haven't had very many since we made our home in Georgia.

I have a thing for snowmen that can be directly traced to my snow-deprived childhood. I grew up in central Texas, where the weather pattern for the year looks like this: Cold— icy—thaw—hot—hot—hotter—hottest—less hot—even less hot—mild—repeat. The cold-to-icy period always occurs in January, and snow just didn't happen in Burnet, Texas. We saw lots of frost and ice, but no snow. So I don't recall ever seeing real snow (other than on TV) until our first trip to Los Alamos, New Mexico, when I was ten years old. It was positively magical. It felt powdery and crunchy under my feet, and it made my heart very happy to walk on it, lie in it, scoop it up, and eat it.

We moved from Texas to Stafford, Virginia, my sophomore year of high school. I think we had been there about six months when I first heard about the possibility of something called a "snow day." You have to understand that this was a concept totally foreign to me, but the prospect made me positively tingly with excitement. As much as I loved going to school (and I did l-o-v-e it; I even tried to convince my mom that I didn't have a fever so that I could get to school when I was contagious), I just knew that if they actually had to cancel classes, the ground would be covered with the magical white fluff.

I had learned from growing up in Texas on the farm that the weatherman was a very important dude, and we had already grown to love our weatherman out of the Washington NBC affiliate station, Mr. Willard Scott. Back before he was on *The Today Show* and announcing all the Very Old People on the graphic replica of the Smucker's jar, he was doing the weather for our nation's capital. Since I lived fifty miles south of D.C. for the rest of high school, Willard Scott was the man who held my snow-day future in his forecast. Every night when there was a possibility of snow, I would pray that the next morning might be the day I would get to stay home and make a snowman or three.

One night we heard Willard say there was a whopper of a storm headed our way and that we needed to tune in for cancellations beginning at 4 a.m. My mom and dad didn't get me up that early, but they did wake me to see something amazing. During the night, the storm had indeed moved in, and the wind had created drifts that reached up to our roof and completely covered the back side of our house. Dad had to actually shovel a path out to the woodpile, and the path had five-*foot*-high snow walls on both sides. It was like I had woken up at the North Pole.

If I ever win a million dollars, I'm sure I won't feel any better than I did when I saw that much snow on *our house*. Since that moment, I have been highly excitable at the prospect of snow in any forecast. It's childish, I know, but I really can't help myself.

Fortunately, John and I lived in Virginia when our children were young, so they've had a taste of snow days for themselves. Living in Georgia now, we must endure the forecaster's tease of a hint of snow once a year—said snow rarely sticking around for more than two hours. It's really just enough to make you frustrated—and we *never* get a White Christmas. Thus, we have our special snowman tribute table. For all the good it's doing us, it might as well be covered with little hula girls.

Back in Virginia, I also learned that Southerners have a big problem understanding the principles of driving in snow. There are rules about snow driving that are second nature to every Minnesotan or Alaskan. You must have all-weather tires that aren't bald, drive only on salted or sanded roads, tap (not stomp on) the brakes, and steer in the same direction you're skidding. These nuances are lost on Southerners—especially the males. They want to show that the snow can't keep them off the streets (stick out chest, hitch up pants). Every Southern man *wants* to go out and drive in the snow, just to prove that he can. However, most of them are abysmal at it and should keep their keister in the house. Southern men need not feel inadequate because of this. Other regions have their issues, too. Southern Californians, for example, cannot drive in the rain.

A classic Christmas movie that is designed around the concept

of snow is the musical *White Christmas*. It is a wonderful production with some fabulous song and dance numbers (if you don't
count the awful one called "Choreography," which is the one we
use as our "advertisement" — the time to go to the kitchen and get
our snacks refilled). But several of the songs are standouts ("Count
Your Blessings Instead of Sheep," for example — if only Bing hadn't
sucked on his pipe the whole time). When Rosemary Clooney,
Vera-Ellen (please tell me she had her spleen or other organs surgi-
cally removed to have a waist that small), Bing Crosby, and Danny
Kaye sing that song about Vermont as they are headed there on the
train, "Snow, snow, snow, snow, snow — I want to wash my hands,
my face and hair with snow," I must sing along — loudly. My children wish I were someone else's mother whenever I do that.

As much as I love snow, I've never really bonded with the
major snow sport, skiing. For some, skiing is an enjoyable, even
exhilarating, form of outdoor exercise. For me, the thought of
being propelled by gravitational forces beyond my control that
cause me to hurtle forward at breakneck speed on slick wooden
planks wearing foggy goggles while trying to avoid natural and
unnatural obstacles with my feet and ankles firmly strapped into
unmovable orthopedic boots and padded by something called a
"bib," with only overgrown toothpicks for balance — well, it's just
not my idea of fun.

Now, my sons took to the sport like fish to water, and John
is an excellent skier himself. The Renfroe men folk love all that
schussing and plowing and moguling. Elyse and I are more like
the Ski Lodge Bunny types. We figure someone needs to stay with

the stuff at the lodge, drink the hot cocoa, and look cute. That would be us.

Not that I haven't tried to ski. Au contraire, I have taken ski lessons several times. I must have had some sort of Ski Skill Inoculation thrown in with my measles, mumps, and rubella vaccinations because I simply cannot master the essential art of snow-plowing. All four of my pretty-boy ski instructors made it sound like any idiot could do it. "Just point your skis together and come to a gradual stop." Sounds simple enough, but my skis had their own idea of where they would like to point.

What the pretty boys failed to mention is that if you happen to sit (read that: *fall*) down on the back of your skis, you cannot "turn" them in *any* direction. At this point you have become, for all intents and purposes, a sled with no steering device. This is how I spent the majority of my time on the mountain: without regard for the lives of the other skiers on the bunny slopes. (I noted that the unsuspecting skiers never take seriously your yelling at them to move until you hit them. *Then* they get all righteous on you.)

In between my spastic attempts to stand back up, I was promising God all sorts of devotion and charitable works if He would just get me off this mountain. The final straw of humiliation was that all the three- and four-year-olds in the Ski Baby Clinic were plowing just fine—even without poles! My paranoia was in full swing as I thought, *They're mocking me!* But it's really hard to assess the full intent of their facial expressions behind those pacifiers.

The ski lift was its own terror. Who thought that it might be a good idea for people to dangle over a mountain on the equivalent of a couple of two-by-fours without a seat belt? Get me back to Six Flags, where they at least strap you in! And there is too much pressure associated with getting *off* the lift. If you lose your courage in the 2.5-second window of opportunity to de-lift, it is too bad, too sad for you. Now you're going even *higher*, where you will have to muster up even *more* courage to leap off, and who can make good decisions at those altitudes?

When I was ten, I didn't hesitate to eat snow. But at my age, I don't exactly relish the thought of my face making sudden and accidental contact with the slope. That's a level of exfoliation I may not need.

Some folks are meant to look good on the slopes; others are meant to be the keepers of the cocoa. I know my place.

riding on the christmas float

Every year on Thanksgiving morning as I am making a heroic effort to get all the menu items ready to eat at the same time (this is the hard part about holiday meals—timing is everything), the little TV on the kitchen counter is tuned to the Macy's Thanksgiving Day Parade. It's been practically immortalized in the classic movie *Miracle on 34th Street* as being *the* place where Santa makes his annual nationwide appearance atop the big float in New York. Of course there are lots of other floats (with pop singers lip-syncing badly, Rockettes dancers kicking hernia-inducing heights, *Today Show* hosts trying to appear enchanted by it all). But the star of the parade is Santa himself.

A whole new category of "holiday float" has arisen in the travel industry over the past decade: the holiday cruise. This vacation option has given all the people who want to make a break with tradition a way to do so Jimmy Buffett style. Their idea is to take all the money they would have spent on gifts for each other and put those resources toward purchasing memories instead. Personally,

I just don't think I would be able to refrain from having some little *something* wrapped up to give, and then that would mess up the whole premise. But I do understand the lure of the cruise brochure.

Before John and I took off on our first oceangoing excursion, I was very much intimidated by the cruise-line advertisements depicted on television. It appeared to me there would be buff, bronze, and beautiful specimens of humanity occupying the high seas with me (me being less than buff, goth-white, and beautiful mostly on the inside). These people had exceptionally white teeth, wore strapless and droopless dresses (well, the girls did), and danced like they were Arthur Murray instructors. Because I wasn't going to get fit in a day, learn to dance in a day, or figure out how to arrange my coconuts in a strapless dress in a day, I was left with only one part of the equation that was within my control. In a moment of insecurity, I decided that I needed a jump start on my "cruise look" by stepping into a Mystic Tan salon to fake my way to the bronze part. It was my first foray into the car-wash approach to tanning, and the perky eighteen-year-old behind the welcome desk could sense my apprehension and tension.

"Don't worry! It's quick and easy. You'll love it."

After I prepaid (smart of them), I followed Miss Perky past the tanning bed room, past the restrooms—far, far away from the front of the building. She took me back to the bronzing room, where the Mystic Tan booth loomed ominously before me, and started to give me the long instruction spiel.

"Now, Mrs. Renfroe, put this shower cap over your hair, but

pull it back one-quarter inch from your hairline and uncover your ears. Then use this moist towelette to remove your makeup. Take this cream and coat your fingernails and toenails individually. Make sure you completely cover each cuticle or they will turn a darker shade of brown than the rest of your skin. When you enter the booth, turn the knob to the tan you desire and push the button to start the motor. You will have three seconds to assume the position before the mist sprays. Close your eyes and stand with your feet shoulder-length apart with your knees slightly bent. Spread your toes and fingers so the mist can get in between them. The spray will be slightly cool, so don't be alarmed. It will spray the front of you for ten seconds and then stop. You'll have five seconds to turn around and assume the next position, which is the same as the first position, with the exception that you must shield the palms of your hands by holding them in front of your belly but leaving the backside of your arms exposed to the wrists to keep the color consistent down the arm. Then the mist will spray for another ten seconds. Try not to breathe in, as it bothers some people's sinuses. Once the mist stops, exit the booth and immediately towel off, starting at your toes and working your way up the body to prevent streaking. Take the moist towelette and wipe your palms as well as in between each finger and toe individually, being careful not to touch your wrists. Do not shower or do any athletic activities for the next four to six hours or your tan will not be uniform. Do you understand, Mrs. Renfroe?"

I nodded my head but secretly wished she had handed me the picture-book version. Somehow "quick" and "easy" were not the terms I would have chosen to describe the bronzing process.

I did all that I could remember of her instructions and stepped (nekkid except for my handy-dandy shower cap) into the Mystic Tan booth. There were more knob options than she had mentioned, so I selected the ones that seemed reasonable. When I pushed the start button and assumed the position, I *was* alarmed by the temperature, which was not the "slightly cool" she described but more like the "Dippin' Dots flash freeze process" I had read about once on an airplane. Some evil (male) designer thought that the "spray warmer" feature was a little too much to ask. Cruel *and* unusual.

As I finished up and got dressed, I noticed a weird smell. I thought maybe it was just the tanning spray in the room, but I noticed I still smelled it while driving my car. It smelled something like old fish food mixed with antifreeze. When I got home, I asked John if he also smelled it. He explained that it was the lovely aroma of the chemicals that were in the self-tanner. (That was *not* in the sales pitch!)

"Mrs. Renfroe, you will be the color of the Coppertone girl and will smell like an opened tuna can. You're gonna love it."

Oh, and the smell lingers for three or four days as it works its way out of your pores. Mmmm — nice. It was a most effective intimacy deterrent.

I needn't have worried about the folks on the cruise resembling those in the television commercials. According to my estimates, the median age of our cruisers was sixty-seven, there was little that was bronze, and "buff" was just the first syllable of their favorite meal style. And these people were not ashamed to let most of it hang out and hang over. I felt like a spring chicken. Smelled like one, too.

One of the greatest attractions of the cruise ship experience was not lost on me. These big boats (aka "Floating Buffets") offer nonstop dining for eighteen-plus hours of each day. If you have late dinner seating (around 8:30 p.m.) you actually finish your evening meal around 10:30 p.m. About that time is when you hear the cruise director come on the overhead speakers and say, "Attention all passengers! Please make your way to the poolside deck on Level 11 for the midnight barbeque and dessert buffet. It starts about an hour from now, so wrap up that last game of bingo and join us for still more food!" In order to keep the female cruisers medicated, the chefs plan chocolate at every meal and even have one midnight buffet that is *entirely* chocolate. The cabin attendants finish off the day by putting chocolates on each pillow. This is all well and good if you don't forget that the chocolate is there and fall asleep with it in your bed. Your body heat can melt those two squares into a big mess.

Until we cruised, I was not aware that you could get sick of the chewing motion and the sight of food in general, but by the end of the week, I just wanted chicken broth through a straw and some lemon water to wash it down. By the way, if you come on the ship a size twelve and leave as a size fourteen, do you have to claim the extra two sizes on your customs form?

Here's a smattering of other notes I made in my mental travelogue while on board. First, my husband and I observed some families with small children around us. We figured out this much: Cruises are no place for children, unless it's a Disney cruise. And a Disney cruise is no place for adults. Therefore, we maintain that the children should go on the Disney cruise and the parents should go on another boat.

Problem solved.

Second, as a rule, women have a habit of going into bathroom stalls and attempting to find seats that have no "sprinkles" on them. Sprinkles are little souvenirs left behind from the stall's former occupant and were created when said occupant was afraid to sit all the way down on the toilet seat for fear of making contact with any sprinkles left behind from the occupant before *her*. It is a self-perpetuating problem. But I have noticed that this is not the case with the cruise ship restrooms. There are *no* sprinkles on those seats. I think it's because the motion of the waves is so strong that no woman can take the anti-sprinkle squatting position and hold it steady when the ship is pitching. She just *has* to sit down.

Another problem solved.

Note also my Tipsy Cruiser Theorem, whereby I postulate that the only people who are able to walk straight on a cruise are the ones who have had too much to drink. Their inability to walk a straight line on land is cancelled out by the action of the seas, so the inebriated walk just fine on the ship.

Finally, you can never quite tell by shore excursion descriptions which ones you should sign up for. They all sound enticing: Jungle Canopy Tour, Horseback Beach Ride, Swim with the Dolphins, Chase the Whales. Chase the whales? Have these people watched

Free Willy one too many times? What if the whales decide to chase you back? Anybody remember The Jonah Incident?

I love the disclaimer on the tour sheet: "We cannot guarantee that you will see any actual whales." Ya think? As if the cruise lines had a couple of trained orcas they could just call up via remote control from the depths to make a special appearance for all the cruisers.

On our cruise, we opted for the Swim and Snorkel Excursion. It promised a boat ride around the rock formations out from the beach of Cabo San Lucas and a chance to view the beautiful aquatic life around them. I donned my swimsuit and cover-up and was ready for action. Now, I'm not exactly what you might term "athletic," but I was fairly sure I could handle doggie paddling around a boat. I was a little apprehensive about the breathing through the snorkel tube, and I had to psyche myself up to breathe in, blow out, breathe in, blow out. But the boat ride out to the rocks was relaxing, and I lost my tension as we rounded the beachfront and the boat slowed down around the rocks. Our guide told us to look at the three rocks jutting out of the water and notice the white caps on them that resemble icing on cupcakes. He informed us that those were not original to the rock but the result of years of buildup of pelican poop. Some things you would just rather not know.

I guess I failed to get the full snorkel memo, because they started passing out gear by giving us the yellow life vests with a little straw attached that you blow into to inflate. The vests had a harness to wrap around your waist and a second strap that comes from the back of your waist through your legs and snaps into the front. I know this design feature was for my safety, but a wedgie was the last thing I needed to distract me from the snorkel breathing pattern.

Our guides then fit us with the fins. I had never had these on my feet in my life, so here was another question of anxiety in my snorkel experience: *How do you swim with the fins?* I was fully prepared to doggie paddle, but fins were a new complication. The next instruction given was to take the snorkel mask and spit into the inside of the eyepiece and smear the saliva around to prevent the glasses from fogging up. *Gross.*

Finally, we were told that the thirty-yard area between where the boat was anchored and the rocks were jutting out of the water was where we could safely snorkel. The time had arrived to get in. I was a-fearin'. *What if I couldn't do it? What if I was a snorkel loser? Would my husband ever look on me with respect again? Would the other cruisers point and snicker at me in the dining room that night?* The raging insecurity made me feel thirteen all over again.

We flipped and flopped our way over to the stairway off the edge of the boat, where our excellent adventure would begin. Our Mexican tour guides failed to mention the teensy, insignificant detail that the water was no more than sixty-five degrees (okay, so it was January, but we thought it was still warmer in Mexican waters), and, as none of us had wet suits, we were immediately channeling a famous scene from the movie *Titanic.* My feet started their frog-swim pattern (it's more like a combination between a doggie paddle and a reptile crawl—it's uniquely my own), but that *doesn't* really work with the fins. As my feet were furiously attempting to do their usual moves to keep me afloat, they seemed to have a mind of their own. The extra twenty-four inches attached to each foot were creating quite a stir in the water while doing nothing to keep me upright or moving in any desired direction. The panic set in.

Between the cold water and the uncooperative fins, I said through my chattering teeth, "John, I don't like this. I want to get back in the boat." My man did not laugh at me (I don't know how he kept from it, though). He said to me, "Anita, you're wearing a life vest, remember? Just relax." Well, duh. Once I stopped my feet from frogging, things improved immediately. At least I lost my fear that I'd trigger a headline in my hometown paper: "Georgia woman drowns while local Mexicans laugh."

So then there was the issue of the mouthpiece. It just wasn't working for me. The saltwater kept getting in it, I still couldn't get the rhythm of "breathe air in, blow water out," and the boat was calling my name. Finally, John realized that I was missing the whole point of this excursion and said, "Anita, just put your face in the water a little and look down." And when I did, *wow!* I got it! There were the most beautiful fish of every color of the rainbow in shapes and sizes that I had seen only on the Discovery Channel. And they were playing around my fins! In those five seconds, I was hooked. Of course, I wanted to let John know I saw the aquatic critters, so I opened my mouth underwater to make a noise about the fish and took in a mouthful of Mexican ocean complete with molecules of pelican poop.

I later thought how much my first snorkeling experience mirrors my feelings about the holiday season. I can get so distracted by the demands and caught up in trying to do it all "right" that I desperately paddle harder, creating a lot of motion but not much progress. I'm so busy managing the equipment that I'm not enjoying anything about the experience. I forget the reason why I was given all this equipment in the first place, and I end up emotionally hyperventilating and wishing the whole thing was over and done with.

All the while, God gently says to me, "Girl, I've got you. I am protecting you, providing for you. Just stop flailing, take a deep breath, and take a look at what's right in front of you. You will see the most amazing things waiting for you just below the surface."

fear knots

There is weirdness in the world that you, Gentle Reader, haven't even imagined. Exhibit de jour: the website www.phobialist. com. Here you will find there's a "-phobia" for just about anything you can imagine. We could all recognize the names of certain fears (arachnophobia—fear of spiders; claustrophobia—fear of enclosed spaces, and so on), but did you know you could have a fearful condition that you don't even realize you have? Here are a few from the website that I did not know were possible:

- Triskaidekaphobia—the fear of the number 13
- Neophobia—fear of anything new
- Peladophobia—fear of bald people
- Ecclesiophobia—fear of church
- Deipnophobia—fear of dinner conversations

I have different kinds of fears than the average person. Some of my personal fears include:

- Indecisiphobia—fear related to my indecision regarding a purchase, so that when I finally make up my mind to get the item, I go back and someone else has already taken it.
- Phonophobia—fear that my cell phone battery will go out and all my stored numbers will have to be reentered (compounded by the fear that I don't have the numbers actually *written down* anywhere).
- Pedopainophobia—fear that the shoes I really love will, in fact, hurt *worse* than I am projecting they may. There have been a few times in my life when I was "sore afraid" (a very accurate biblical term).

If you are suddenly overcome with a wave of fear, it can do things to you physically. My normal adrenal/fear response includes that warm sensation starting at the top of my head simultaneous with a cold, clammy feeling in my extremities. Add to that the usual knots that develop in the pit of my stomach (as if it weren't already lumpy enough).

I am not generally a claustrophobic person (I did survive an MRI for my neck, and I've heard that if you can make it through one of those, you are not claustrophobic). But during a trip to Egypt a few years ago, I could certainly relate to those who are. My husband and I, my mom and dad, and a group from our church spent three days touring the ancient city of Cairo, and our first day was spent viewing the countryside and doing a little shopping. There are many things available there for "one American dollar, pretty lady," but none that I felt justified the space in my suitcase. I did get a cartouche ring that sported my three initials in hieroglyphics (they are, interestingly enough, an eagle, a mouth, and a basket—I thought that a "high strung verbal basket case" was pretty accurate). We also kicked around the Cairo Museum of Antiquities and saw some amazing displays from King Tut's tomb. What was of greatest interest to me, though, was the fact that the many artifacts and sculptures over three thousand years old were not encased or surrounded by anything that would protect them. You could walk right up and touch them! Contrast this with the United States, where George Washington's two-hundred-year-old dentures are hermetically sealed and roped off to prevent damage.

My brush with claustrophobia occurred on our day trip to the Pyramids. We somehow decided it would be a great idea to ride a camel from the tour bus area over to the Pyramids. In the souvenir stores, the small stuffed camels look friendly and cute. On the brochure, the photographed camels look large and friendly and cute. In reality, these animals smell worse than a Roto-Rooter drill bit, make sounds louder and stranger than Chewbacca, and have learned their manners from two-year-olds (they spit and bite). Not to mention that the camel gallop makes a horse trot feel like a ride in a Cadillac.

We rode our camels across the desert sands like "Ahab the Arab" and prayed they wouldn't whip their necks around and bite a chunk out of our ankles. I kissed the ground upon dismount, sand notwithstanding.

Directly following the camel trauma, we were to make our way into the heart of a pyramid to see a burial chamber. We all reeked of camel and felt itchy, hot, and sandy. I don't know why I thought this would be a good idea. (It's like someone saying to you, "Hey, I know what let's do for fun! Let's go visit an ancient indoor mausoleum that has been inaccessible for years on purpose! It'll be a blast!") But my dad, my husband, and I reasoned, "We're only in Cairo once, so let's do everything on the brochure."

The opening to the first pyramid looked nonthreatening enough. It was tall and wide enough to accommodate two adults side by side, and there was no indication that inside it would be any other way. What we could not know is that once inside a dozen yards or so, the entryway begins to narrow considerably and starts to shrink vertically. You can't tell exactly how far you have to go to the crypt because the passageway only grows darker and darker, narrower and narrower.

We had gone about thirty yards into the darkness when the tunnel narrowed to the point that we were practically duck-walking. It was uncomfortable for me, but I felt especially bad for my six-foot-five husband, who was cramped up like a camel in a pet carry-on crate. I felt my heart racing, and my instincts told me to turn around and head back toward the light, but there wasn't even room to turn around! And when I looked back at the rectangle of glaring sunlight, it seemed to be very far away. I had no choice but to keep going forward into the unknown.

Just when it seemed I couldn't breathe at all, the narrow opening dumped us into a dark, dank chamber. The relief that washed over me to be out of that tunnel is inexpressible. But I must be honest when I tell you that while I was expecting a room of wonders for all my labor to arrive there, it was only a small space with a rectangular chamber where someone dead had previously spent some significant time. It was most definitely *not* worth the camel-and-tunnel journey. I thought it would be nice if someone would rewrite the Pyramid Excursion brochure to read, "Camels mean and stinky. Pyramids a claustrophobic nightmare. Not much to see. Save your money."

While I was visiting the phobia website, I noticed there aren't any associated with Christmas, although I have a few that I think should have made the list:

- Visanegaphobia—the fear you experience while awaiting the approval code on your credit card purchase as you imagine you might be declined due to over-limit issues. This fear causes you to look at the ceiling or stare at your shoes until the approval comes through.
- Pyrexaphobia—a fear that you will never get your casserole dish returned to you from the neighborhood holiday party.
- Ribbonknotaphobia—the fear that there will be no scissors handy when you are trying desperately to *politely* unwrap the gift your mother-in-law festooned with eight yards of tightly tied curly garland.

I recently heard that there are 365 "fear nots" in the Bible. (That's what you get for believing everything you hear in sermons. I just looked it up, and there are only 128—and that's counting the "be not afraids.") Most of us are acquainted with some of the biggies, such as God telling Joshua not to be afraid to take on the fortress of Jericho, and Jesus telling His disciples not to fear as He was walking on the water toward them. And, of course, there are the infamous "fear nots" associated with the Christmas story.

An angel told Mary not to be afraid of the message or the method by which God's Son would enter this realm. An angel told Joseph that he didn't have to be afraid that Mary was trippin' when she informed him that she was the first and only known case of divine artificial insemination. And a heavenly host told the shepherds not to freak out at their announcement but to take a break from the sheep thing to go visit the Great Shepherd. Apparently, there were many things that God didn't want humans to fear. The angels were giving the message "Chill, y'all" (that's Georgiaese) to everyone to whom they appeared. Maybe it's in *The Angel Handbook*: "When you approach mortals, begin with a greeting of 'Fear not,' as humans have an entire website devoted to listing all the things they are afraid of."

But there was one person that an angel told Mary and Joseph *to* fear, and that was Herod. Because of Herod's insane jealousy and intent to find Jesus and murder Him, Mary and Joseph took Jesus to Egypt for awhile. Joseph may have taken Jesus on a camel ride past the Pyramids while they were visiting, although I'm sure they didn't have brochures or tour guides back then.

The ratio of "fear nots" to "fear" informs our faith. Some fears are irrational and diminish us. These are also the ones that tend to occupy the most real estate in our heads. Then there are a few well-founded cautions that need to be heeded for our own safety.

My problem is that I have trouble distinguishing between the two types of fear.

I'm learning to run my response through the love and wisdom tests. The Bible tells us that "perfect love drives out fear" (1 John 4:18), so I practice asking myself if my thoughts are directed by love. The second test of a fear is whether or not it contains the voice of wisdom. Proverbs 1:7 tells us, "The fear of the LORD is the beginning of knowledge." (I think fleeing to escape a murderous dictator would fit into that category.) Some cautions are just common sense. I think of the scene in the movie *Bruce Almighty* when Jim Carrey's character finally submits to God's authority in his life and is immediately hit by a Mack truck. When Bruce asks God (portrayed by Morgan Freeman) how this could happen while he was praying, God replies, "You can't kneel down in the middle of the street and not expect to get hit by a truck." *Hello!*

What are your fears this holiday season? This week? This moment? Do they pass the love and wisdom tests? If not, lose the fear knots.

Follow the advice of the Christmas angels: "Chill, y'all."

and you made this yourself?

If you take a roomful of thirty female test subjects and hook them up to pulse monitors and all the little diodes that measure emotional response to different words and one of those words is *handcrafts*, the response ratio would probably fall into three distinct categories. One-third of the women would be repulsed by the idea, one-third of the test subjects would have no measurable response, and one-third would begin openly salivating. Women in this third category believe that if instructions exist for any project, they can make it. I should have known that I was not in this category when I had to have a friend reinstall my zipper on my final-grade project for my seventh-grade home economics class. (Why does it matter if the zipper doesn't zip *up* to the closed position, as long as it closes? Home ec teachers have no imagination.)

I must confess that my teenage experience did not clue me in and I devoted many holiday seasons of my adulthood to making crafty Christmas gifts. This was, in part, because John and I were inordinately un-wealthy for the first ten years of our marriage. I've heard people wax nostalgic for the happiness they felt when they were young and in love, poor but happy. Not me. I have a Technicolor recollection of the Sonic burgers, Frito chili pies, and tater tots. The resulting gastric distress is an element of "young, poor, and in love" that I do not miss. We were this level of poor because we had mucho student loans, babies and their accoutrement, and the reality that most churches don't believe in paying youth pastors much money. I don't blame them. Youth work is far too much fun to get paid well. You know what a joy it is to take forty-seven teenagers to camp, right? And lock-ins? Who doesn't volunteer to supervise those? We keep wondering when the "wealth" part of our lives is going to kick in. We have come to think of our kids-in-college stage as "a higher level of broke."

But back in the day, I would start in September planning my crafty forays for the fall. I would quest for the types of crafts I could do successfully (I cannot paint or sew anything more than a straight line, so my options were limited). I used to (I am not making this up — there are witnesses) drive an hour to the Moormont Apple Orchard, pick apples, take them home, slice them thin with a deli meat slicer, dip them in salt water with lemon juice added (to keep them from turning dark), lay them on drying screens in a warm oven with a wooden spoon wedging the oven door open, leave them there overnight, turn them in the morning to finish fully drying them, and then take them out for stringing between dried orange slices, drilled whole nutmegs, and dried whole bay leaves. The energy this required was an amount I will never experience again. Does this behavior officially qualify as insanity? What on earth made me think this was a great use of my time? It must have been all the *Country Living* magazines extolling the charms of the country life, replete with beeswax candles, lye soap, and knotty pine furniture. I should have bought different magazines.

I also made such wondrous crafts as cinnamon/applesauce/glue ornaments (rolled out and cut into cookie shapes), hanging dolly heads (made out of cornstarch, baking soda, and water, rolled into balls, baked until hard, faces painted on, straw hair glued on), and rosebud topiaries (if you glue 765 dried rosebuds to a Styrofoam ball, you can cover it completely, but *why?*).

Some of my extraordinarily crafty friends would organize a craft show around Thanksgiving time to make money for purchasing Christmas gifts. We were ahead of our time in the concept of multitasking, as the things left from the show were our ready-made inventory for fulfilling our own Christmas lists for friends and family. For all my friends and family who received these items and thought they were lame but were kind enough to display them in prominent areas of their homes when I came to visit, I offer this public apology and thank you for loving me enough to compromise your décor.

Sometimes we craft sellers would trade things between our tables in order to have a greater variety of things to give to the people on our Christmas list. That was tricky since some items were more desirable than others and you had to seem enthused about trading for the lesser desirables. How do you finesse that situation amongst friends? There was one girl who was a great painter and we *all* wanted her stuff. I think I fell somewhere in the middle of the food chain, as my stuff wasn't the best, but it wasn't the worst, either. What none of us realized was that if we hadn't spent so much money on raw materials for the crafts, we could have had money to buy Christmas presents for everyone on our lists—you know, gifts they actually wanted. This wisdom slipped past us somehow.

But Christmas is a time when even the Far-Less-Than-Crafty feel an inexplicable compulsion to try their hand at the Homemade Gift Category. Maybe it's psychologically ingrained from all those ornaments we made as children. When we smell pine trees brought indoors and see the decorations in the store windows, we have the uncontrollable desire to reach for the glue, glitter, and scissors. We are like zombies mindlessly drawn toward the craft store to do things we would not do any other time of the year. And the results are mixed. If your friends have to *ask* you what it is, you might have missed the mark. I say, if no one has affirmed you in this area previously, you might be better off leaving it alone.

Some of my friends give culinary gifts. They spend hours in their kitchens preparing homemade jellies or gourmet vinegars presented in lovely jars with printed labels or home-baked breads with flavored oils. It became apparent to me that my crafty gifts weren't getting the same level of response as in years past, so one year I switched over to gifts of food. Maybe I was just hungry. Whatever the reason, food seemed to be a basic human need and not as likely to clash with someone's wallpaper.

I scoured the recipe books for something novel and found a few recipes for biscotti (for those who do not frequent Starbucks, these are basically doggie biscuits for people—hard, crunchy, promote strident chewing). I baked a quantity of them in several flavors, found clear corsage boxes, placed a paper doily on the bottom, filled each box with biscotti, and tied the whole thing up with some lovely fabric ribbon. I was sure that I had hit upon the perfect food gift. These dehydrated Italian sweet biscuits are in all the coffee shops these days, but back in 1993, I found myself having to explain to the confused recipient exactly what they were.

"They're Italian. They're *supposed* to be dried out. Yes, on purpose."

I might have been slightly ahead of my time, but the truth is that most of my friends and family didn't really want a variety pack of human doggie biscuits to have with their coffee no matter how cute the packaging.

My last experiment in homemade gifts involved sugar bath products. After strolling through a bath and body store and reading the ingredient list on one of their eighteen-dollar sugar scrubs, I felt certain I could replicate their formula for a lot less money (that is precisely the sort of thinking that always gets me in trouble). This was one I should have left to the professionals.

I trekked to the health food store (aka Most Expensive Place to Purchase Anything) and bought raw sugar (turbinado), almond and avocado oil, and assorted essential oils for scenting. I also spent money on containers with strong seals (you wouldn't want the oil leaking onto the shower floor, thereby creating a chance for disaster). I was set. The mixing of the sugar scrubs was a wonderful experience (my hands were never so soft—an added bonus), and the packaging was no problem, either. I will just leave you with the lesson that I learned from this homemade gift: No matter how tight the seal seems to be, ants like sugar scrub, too.

So, my friends, I leave it up to you to decide if you are truly crafty or just a wannabe. Look for clues in your recipients' responses and comments:

- Do they smile wanly as they turn the item a full 360-degree rotation?
- Do they make general comments such as, "Well, would you look at that?"
- Do they close their eyes while mentally grasping for any adjectives to describe it?
- Do they accidentally/on purpose "forget" their present when they are leaving?

If so, you may need to come to terms with your less-than-craftiness. Don't think of it as a journey away from the craft store so much as a journey toward your true nature. We can't all be great at the handmade gift or there would be no need for the mall.

gifts that keep on giving

Last Christmas my mom got a family gift for us. It was a battery-operated pepper mill. When you press the button on top, the mill makes a lovely whirring sound and sends a mist of finely ground pepper onto your waiting entrée. It is a little mechanical marvel, but it caused me to wonder: *Exactly how lazy are we that we can't turn the twist top on a pepper mill to grind our pepper? We wouldn't want to exert ourselves unnecessarily, would we?*

While browsing a catalog recently, I saw a ceramic ice-cream-cone holder that had a battery-operated twirler built right in. I suppose this is so you wouldn't have to turn your wrist to put the perfect lick on it. This is almost as bad as the radio controls built into the steering wheels of late-model cars. We have somehow decided that leaning forward two inches to extend our finger to the position where the radio controls used to be is just too much trouble.

In every family unit, there are people who are the gift "idea" people and those who are the "go out and retrieve the item that the idea person thought up" people. I fall into the "idea" category.

I envision a great gift for someone and then send John out to find it if I can't order it online. This was especially handy when the kids were little, since I have an allergy to toy stores. Even toy departments in discount stores give me hives. I recall being in a Toys R Us store only once in all the years that my kids were little. Something about the smell of all that plastic causes me to have a meltdown, and I just want to get outta there. John, conversely, ever the kid at heart, loved to go in there and test the toys out—you know, "just to be sure that it's something the kids will like." Right.

I've also never understood the people who were hung up on the concept of "educational toys." I have friends who would quest for weeks to find the perfect toy that would raise their child's IQ by several points. And isn't it interesting that anything labeled "educational" will cost a *lot* more money? It has been my experience that the "educational" toys will usually languish in the toy chest while the kids happily bang wooden spoons on cookware. My theory on "educational toys" is this: They're for *children*. At this stage of life, *everything* is educational.

And this is fact, not theory: A child's attraction to any toy will be directly proportional to the amount of annoying sounds said toy makes. It's a conspiracy between the toy manufacturers and the pain reliever companies.

When Austin was two years old, he had a red plastic riding toy that looked like a tractor. It had wheels in the front and back and was skinny enough that he could sling a leg over it and scoot it all around the house. One night when I was out, John was upstairs giving both the boys a bath. He had just finished drying off Austin and was getting Calvin out of the tub when he heard a thump, thump, thump, followed by a loud crash at the bottom of the stairs. He raced around the corner to see Austin sprawled out, naked as the day he was born, looking quite stunned with his tractor by his side. Seems that Austin thought it would be fun to ride his tractor down the stairs. John rushed to Austin's side, afraid he had broken a bone or might be bleeding, but it seemed Austin was more stunned than hurt. So John held Austin for a minute, got him dressed, and went back to tend to Calvin. He immediately heard another thumping sound, but this time it was Austin trying to drag his tractor back up the stairs to take another ride down. These are the male genes that women do not understand.

Our kids loved anything motorized. We had all manner of vehicles that had to be charged overnight. The boys had motorized three-wheelers they would ride through the house, and Elyse had her prized Barbie Jeep. She wouldn't let anyone else drive it, so in all of our pictures of her in her Jeep, she is chauffeuring someone. She also had a "My Size Barbie" when she was five years old. The only problem was that it wasn't "her" size. The thing was at least a foot taller, and she couldn't sleep with the "toy" in the room with her, as it scared her. We were not surprised when we discovered this doll-on-steroids with a bad haircut and permanent marker on her face. Elyse had spoken.

As our kids' ages have increased, so has the cost of their "toys." Computers and MP3 players and cameras and cell phones are now the items that top their lists. If only we could get them excited about a Barbie Jeep again. But we always deposit a few gift cards for a national chain of electronics stores in their stockings so they can indulge their need for all things programmed.

The rise of the gift card and gift certificate on America's Christmas list is Exhibit A regarding twenty-first-century logic. The range of things that receiving a gift card *could* mean is vast:

"I know you love to shop and I knew this would make you happy."

Or

"I wanted to get you something but didn't want to go to a lot of trouble."

Or

"I wanted to give you a present, but I don't really know your taste and didn't want to risk getting you something that would result in one of those, 'Oh, how nice,' moments."

Or

"You're just too difficult to shop for."

Or

"I *didn't* get you anything, but I had these emergency gift cards stashed away just in case someone like you popped up on the Christmas list."

Or

"I didn't *want* to get you anything, and this is as close as I could get to nothing."

It's hard to say which message a gift card might carry. I suppose it depends on who gives it to you. But for the parent of teenagers or young adults with constantly shifting tastes, gift cards are an answer to prayer. We know that our kids will have a great time getting something we won't have to return.

Personally, I really love receiving gift cards because I consider shopping a sport of sorts. You have a "goal" in mind as you shop, you must "beat out" the other shoppers to the one thing left in your size, and you "score" when you find something you really need on sale. When they start a TV channel that features world-class shopping competitions with corporate sponsors and commentators, I'll TiVo that in a heartbeat.

One of the greatest things about gift cards is that they are a virtually effortless regifting commodity. Regifting is also a sign of the times, and it requires meticulous record keeping. You have to write down who the gift is from and whether it has any personalization (how bad would *that* be). If you are going to regift it, you have to be certain it goes to someone in another geographic region who has absolutely no personal connection to the person who gave it to you. This is all so tricky that almost no one has done it successfully more than once.

One item that is a sure bet to get regifted is almost any article of jewelry (other than actual diamonds—you can hardly go wrong with those). Jewelry gifts are risky because you might think you know people's taste, but you may only know what they *used* to like. The fashion trends change so quickly that the things they wear now aren't the things they aspire to wear in the future, and that means they are going to have to *pretend* to like it in your presence and then stick it in their regift pile. They will regift it to someone whose jewelry taste they are only guessing at, and that recipient will pretend to like it in their presence and then add it to her regift pile. It may eventually work its way back into the hands of the original purchaser through the long, winding path of the regifting process. I suggest making a special mark on the back of the card the jewelry is attached to just so you'll know it's the same one.

It is safe to regift if the item in question is a gag gift or a running joke. My husband and his friend Jim had a great tradition of giving each other the same hideous pair of thongs every Christmas. No, not the Victoria's Secret kind, although those might be more comfortable if they were like these: black, furry, and padded. This was one tricked-out pair of flip-flops. They were man-sized but not manly. In fact, they had a 1975 rainbow stripe piece that went between the toes and held the shoe on the foot. Like I said, they were hideous.

It became a yearly tradition for the person who received the flip-flops to add something gaudy to them and give them back to the other guy. Then that person would add something gaudier to them and regift them the next year. By the time we moved away, those shoes had tinsel, lights, mistletoe, ribbons, jingle bells, and lace. Good times.

Why don't we start a campaign to do away with the social stigma associated with regifting? Is it truly a gift-giving shame, or is it a brilliant form of recycling? I mean, haven't we all been the recipients of a gift that, once opened, made us immediately think two things:

1. This is *so* not me.
2. But this would be perfect for _____.

If we can find a warm, loving, accepting home for these errant gifts, wouldn't that make the world a better place?

Just remember to remove the original "to___/from___" sticker until the rest of the world catches up.

the easy-bake oven diaries

I don't have a great memory. I don't know if I'm so scattered that I don't pay enough attention to adequately catalog events in my mind or if my memory banks just get erased while I'm sleeping, but my family is always recounting things in great detail that I can barely recall happening. My first inclination is to think they are setting me up for the opportunity to put me away by making me think I've lost my mind. (If I've slept since the event in question occurred, something *was* lost.)

I've since become more philosophical about my slipping memory. My current mantra is, "If you love a thought, set it free. If it was really yours to begin with, it will come back to you. If it doesn't come back, now there's more room for other thoughts." I'm thinking I once thought of making it into a greeting card for the forgetful, but I can't remember if I thought it was a good idea or not.

But in my holiday memory bank, there are a couple of Christmases in my childhood that stand out in great detail to me. One is the year I got my first bike, complete with a banana seat and plastic streamers. I think it was the Christmas that I was six and still believed in Santa Claus. We lived with my grandparents out in the country, and our roads were dark and winding. My uncle Lewis came over and convinced me that if I went for a drive down Mormon Mill Road with him, we might spot Santa and his sleigh, as some of the neighbors had reported seeing him in the area. Well, I was standing right there beside myself with excitement, and I ran out the door with the absolute knowledge that I was about to see Santa's sleigh with my very own eyes. We drove down the dark roads, and I got so close to the windshield that my breath fogged it up.

"Now, you keep your eyes peeled for that sleigh," Lewis instructed.

The power of suggestion is a strong psychotic force, as I truly believed I caught a glimpse of Santa at least twice during that ride. The journey took about ten minutes, and soon we were back at the ranch (literally). I burst through the door to tell my mother I had seen the sleigh, but she started talking first.

"Anita, you'll never believe what just happened! You just missed him. Santa came while you were out, but he left you this bike."

That might have been my first experience with seriously conflicting emotions. I was simultaneously crushed that I had missed him coming to my very own house but speechless at the utter coolness of this bike. Banana seats were the newest, hippest feature that one could have on one's bike, and I was in possession! I immediately concluded that possessing a banana seat trumped witnessing a personal visit from Santa and went to sleep secure in the knowledge that I had, indeed, seen him through the fog of Uncle Lewis's windshield.

There is also a photo of me that same Christmas as I sat on a floor with my knees bent and my feet sticking out on each side. I can't begin to recreate that position today, but I recall spending a great deal of my childhood sitting like that on the floor. Flexibility is wasted on the young.

I sat there with some striped slipper socks on my feet, my hair in a headband, and a doll with open-and-shut eyes on my lap. I treasure this picture, as it is one of the only photographic remembrances I have of anything remotely girly in my young life. I was surrounded by boy cousins, and most of my playtime was spent with Tonka trucks, miniature front-end loaders, green plastic soldiers, and Hot Wheels. Out in the country, our playtime was spent doing almost everything outside. We squished a lot of Chinaberries, watched a lot of trash burn (we had a chicken-wire cylinder about five feet high and five feet wide, where we dumped our trash and burned it down once a week—this is countrified waste management), and did lots of daring. I have a very distinct scar on my right leg that reminds me of when my cousin and I were playing a game that involved jumping over a low piece of barbed wire to see who could do it the most. I lost. So it was that Barbies were not on my radar, and my one dolly was a treasure—until my boy cousins beheaded her.

The Christmas of my ninth year was a standout, too. My mom was dating my future stepfather, the world looked rosier in general, and I received presents that featured electrical cords. This must've been the first year anyone believed that I could utilize a plug-in item without electrocuting myself. But the standards of risk management were different then. We didn't have seat belt laws, our schools were built with asbestos, there was lead in the wall paint of our rooms, *and* we drank tap water. How did we ever survive?

That was the year I got a Lite-Brite and an Easy-Bake Oven. Life was good. I was gonna cook *and* make light-up art. I was moving up on the girly Maslow Hierarchy of Needs Chart. The Lite-Brite came with black paper templates to help you make something recognizable (although they only worked once, so if you came up with something you liked, you would leave it up for a week or two, as you knew you could never replicate it). But my favorite artistic method was to freestyle. I would spell words and make my own designs. Occasionally the Lite-Brite pegs would get stuck in the holes and break as you were pulling them out. That was particularly troublesome when you would get down to the end of a design and run out of the color you needed to finish it. Because we lived in the country in the days before Internet shopping, Lite-Brite replacements were just not gonna happen.

Neither were replacement mixes for the Easy-Bake Oven. You have to hand it to whoever decided you could put a lightbulb in a painted piece of plastic and pawn it off as a miniature oven. It certainly worked on me. I saw those commercials on Saturday morning cartoons and knew that if I had that oven, my eyes would fly open wider than that girl's on the TV as I took the special tool and slid my mini-cake out the other side. Wouldn't I be the envy of all my boy cousins?

What I didn't realize was that the "mini" part was all too true, and the fifteen minutes that you had to wait for the cake to cook was ten times longer than the cake would last around my cousins. They didn't even let me frost it! And once the three mixes included with the oven were history, so was the usefulness of my much-coveted appliance. Such details were never articulated on the commercial. The nearest store that had more mixes was fifty miles away in Austin.

Bummer.

The Easy-Bake Oven taught me some great life lessons that are still with me today:

- Commercials are powerful.
- Nothing is quite as good as it looks in a commercial.
- If you stick a small item (such as a ring or a dollar) into an Easy-Bake Oven to hide it from your boy cousins and it falls through the baking rack into the bottom, you will never get it out.

santa's ebay sleigh

Imagine with me, if you would, that an international bazaar has opened right near your home. You can shop there any time of the day or night, as it's open 'round the clock. It's a very large store with almost anything you could imagine for sale inside, and it seems like the answer to your prayers for finishing up your Christmas shopping because there is, truly, something for everyone. There are yachts for sale alongside half a grilled cheese sandwich shaped like the Virgin Mary. The only catch is that there are no *actual items* in the store — just photographs lying on the tables with the owners of the items standing near the photo, ready to describe it to you (only in generalities). These people have large brown bags over their heads so you can't tell if you're dealing with a granny from Indiana or a shyster from Malaysia.

The bazaar seems like a yard sale, except instead of haggling the owner down to a lower price, it is an auction where the prices only go up as other people decide they want the same item you do. In fact, there is a timer on the table next to the picture of the item and it is counting down from the moment the item is made available. The availability of any item you are interested in could expire while you are gone to work, sleeping, or in the shower, so you have to have someone call to tell you when your item is going off the table. This is fine when you are interested in only one thing, but in time you become addicted to the unlimited availability of so many things at such great prices that you are juggling dozens of items at once. As the timer nears expiration, people start circling the table and incrementally driving the price up. The bidding war escalates to a frenzy. You really want this item, but your doubts start creeping in:

> *Is this photo truly depicting what I will be getting?*
> *Can I trust the seller's description?*
> *Is the price too much already, or should I go higher with my bid?*
> *Will the item arrive unharmed to me by the time I need it?*

So as the five Really Serious Buyers continue bidding for the last two minutes, your palms get sweaty, your mouth goes dry, and you try to figure out how much you are willing to pay in the heat of the moment. At the very last second, right before you are sure you have bid high enough to secure the item for your very own, a very savvy collector from Denmark swoops in and outbids you by a dollar. Timer goes off. Game over.

Welcome to eBay.

The above scenario is pretty accurate, except the virtual bazaar comes to you via your modem or DSL, and you can bid 24/7/365 in your own pajamas.

For hundreds of years, the manner by which we exchanged goods and services was much the same. Listen while I tell you of the way that shopping happened for centuries:

1. Somewhere, someone had a store of some sort with goods that you wanted or needed.
2. You would find out about the product and place of business and go there to look over said merchandise.
3. You would determine the worth of the merchandise and whether it met a need in your life.
4. a) You would give the owner some sort of payment and bring this merchandise to your house where
   b) you would immediately regret ever having bought it.

The World's Largest Yard Sale (aka eBay) eradicates all of the above steps except for 4b.

There was a time when I would check my eBay "Items I Am Watching" page several times per day. Yea, verily, I have been an eBay addict. It started when I found out I could find really inexpensive frames for my glasses. I discovered a source in Florida who has lots of funky eyeglass frames, and I have bought several from her eBay store. Then I moved on to other things, like my favorite bathing salts (seemed like a good idea at the time, but they are heavy and cost a lot to ship), hard-to-find books (sometimes cheaper than Amazon), a couple of rings (good deals on silver!), and the car I am currently driving.

You think I'm kidding, but I'm not. I wanted an older Jaguar body (on the car, not on me) in the color red. I spent the better part of the past ten years carting my kids from place to place in a Suburban, and Mama was ready to ride a little lower for a while. After talking to a few reliable sources, the consensus seemed to be that Jaguar engines are temperamental and expensive to repair, so I figured that the red, decade-old Jag also needed to be retrofit with an American engine and in good shape.

This was a pretty specific order, wouldn't you say? Lo and behold, after entering my keywords in the search engine, said coveted item popped up in south Atlanta. Within a few hours I was down there test-driving it before the bidding opened. I did not win the actual bidding, but the other bidder fell through, and the car was mine, mine, mine. Where else but on eBay? That's not to say that it didn't turn out to be a long-term-project car, but I do look *very* good sitting in it on the side of the road whenever I am waiting for the tow truck.

The concept of eBay and the service it provides is quite remarkable. The legend is that some techie built the computer program that runs eBay because his girlfriend was having a hard time finding people in her geographic region to trade with while she quested to expand her Pez dispenser collection. He felt the time had come to harness the global nature of the Internet for his beloved's desires. Talk about a technical Taj Mahal! eBay exists due to the fact that someone finally figured out that because of digital photography and Internet access, *no one* should be denied the opportunity to buy anyone's stuff from anywhere on the planet.

There is even a book about a guy who sold everything he

owned on eBay. His book, which catalogs this experience, is called *All My Life for Sale*. Author John D. Freyer tells of how he sold *everything* he owned (including a half-empty bottle of mouthwash, an unopened box of taco shells, and a Ziploc baggie with his sideburns in it) on eBay and then proceeded to go visit all his stuff all over the world. I don't understand why, but someone somewhere paid money for all the flotsam of this guy's life. That's why I refer to eBay as the World's Largest Yard Sale, because a yard sale is a wondrous marriage between bargain hunters and a seller's discards. When your old stuff finds a good home, it's very satisfying. But I've never had the urge to ask for the buyer's address so that I can come and visit my stuff later.

Now whenever I am at a store contemplating the purchase of any new item, I try to envision myself several years into the future, standing in my yard, attempting to convince a friendly shopper that this well-used item is worth at least two-thirds of the price I paid for it. If I can't see it as a winner in the secondary market, I don't buy it.

If you are new to the eBay experience, I have some hard-won lessons to share with you before you dive in:

1. *Don't even go near it if you have an addictive personality.* There is something very hypnotic about this shopping-without-borders experience. You will find yourself lured into the World Wide Web like an unsuspecting fly. It won't seem like a big-time commitment at first, but eventually you will spend hours checking

on the new items that have become available since the last time you checked in as well as the current prices of the five items you are watching, surfing in new categories, and adding searches to your "favorites." Many people think they are saving time by shopping this way, but in reality you will spend more time surfing eBay than you would spend walking the whole mall twice over. There will also be the telltale signs of the eBay Eyes—bloodshot and bleary—and the urge to close your browser window when other people enter the room so that they won't know how much time you're spending at the online bazaar. Be forewarned: There is no known twelve-step recovery program for eBay addicts.

2. *Learn to decode the descriptions.* Do you remember your first home-purchase experience? How you would read the ad for a house and be so very excited about it, only to find out that the description was accurate only if you knew the fine art of reading real estate ads? You know how it read "fixer-upper" and it really meant "falling-downer"? Well, eBay is much the same.

    "nostalgic" = "old"

    "unusual" = "weird"

    "well loved" = "bad shape"

    "too many features to describe here" = "we don't really know how it works"

3. *Don't bid if you don't have a price limit in mind.* The emotional factor to *win* the bidding war will take you

places you never intended to go. You have to know how much you are willing to spend before the bidding starts or you will get caught up in the thrill of the chase and end up flat busted over an item you're not even sure you want. Write down a number you think is fair (don't forget the shipping—a washing machine for $1 is not a great deal if you have to pay $550 to get it shipped to you) and stick to it. If you have ever been to the fair and spent $69 trying to win a $3 stuffed animal, stay far, far away from eBay.

4. *If you don't have DSL, you will lose every bid.* Dial-up is not your friend on eBay. The more experienced bidders wait until the last possible second to "slam" in their bid. If you have dial-up, you're out.

5. *Beware all quick-delivery promises.* If you are Christmas shopping and it's a r-e-a-l-l-y important gift, just know there are some seriously slow shippers out there and your children will *not* understand if Santa's eBay Sleigh is held up by problems in transit.

give and take

We have all heard the saying "It is more blessed to give than to receive." Because Jesus himself actually said it, I've really tried to help my kids get a handle on this concept. But it's one that is radically countercultural, as are most of the concepts that Jesus came to live out among us.

When Elyse was about four years old (before she understood the whole Christmas gift thing), she took one of Austin's favorite toys and wrapped it up and gave it to him. She was so proud because she knew he liked it. Her heart was in the right place, but he still brings it up more than a dozen years later.

When our kids were young, they participated in an AWANA Club (where they got to have lots of fun learning about God and the Bible). They would earn Awana Bucks to spend at the Awana Store (a room set up in the church stocked with donated items) and then purchase small gifts with the tokens they received for memorizing Scripture and winning team competitions. The kids enjoyed giving the gifts they had earned, but the items were generic and could have been appropriate for just about anyone. I am happy to report that my kids have moved past the stage of getting something for someone just to mark that person off their shopping list and are beginning to take joy in choosing gifts that are a great expression of the interests and passions of the recipient.

Last Christmas Austin gave his father an elaborately technical remote control that makes all the other eight remotes unnecessary. It was the perfect gift for John, as he had begun the scary first step toward the nursing home: muttering when he can't find the correct remote. This gadget is just a couple of hiccups away from Artificial Intelligence, and it even lights up when you walk past it. Personally, that scares me because I know how much John loves it, and frankly I'm not sure I can compete with something that lights up *every single time* he walks by. But to the men folk in our household, this is a technological wonder that is highly revered. Austin thought of John's needs and found something that was a perfect fit for him.

Calvin bought John a "How to Fix (just about) Everything" encyclopedia. It has over five hundred entries from "How to zap an acne breakout" to "How to mend a family feud" to "How to stop an ant invasion." And Elyse got her dad a gift card to the movies so that he could indulge his appetite for shoot-em-up flicks. It's great to watch the kids develop their own ideas about what constitutes a thoughtful, well-chosen gift—not because it reflects well on them but because it brings happiness to the heart of the one who receives it.

The Bible is full of stories that celebrate generosity and

principles that teach us that the joy of giving is to be a calling card of our life. "God loves a cheerful giver," Paul told the early Christians (2 Corinthians 9:7). But he also stressed that God seems more concerned with the heart's motivation than with the actual gift. I guess that would be logical since He's God and already owns everything.

What surprises me more is the Bible's many references to what God would have us *take.* Over and over we read that certain things are there for the taking if only we will:

- Take courage
- Take joy
- Take hold
- Take heart
- Take refuge
- Take delight

These seem to be categories in which the predicating principle is that we have the faith to step forward and take these things we so desperately need. But isn't that the nature of God's love toward us? To hold out everything we need and say, "Take it! It's for you because I love you."

During this Christmas season, may I remind you of some things that are yours for the taking?

1. *Take a little time.* Would you pause for a moment to find a writing implement and make a list of people whose

love and belief in you have made a real, lasting impact on your life? It doesn't have to be a long list—maybe four or five names. As you are writing the names down, recall how those people's encouragement made the life you are now living a reality.

Now take that same writing implement and note out to the side of each name how you intend to contact the person in the next seven days to express your gratitude. Do not wait. Hasn't it taken you long enough already? If you have held your gratitude in your heart and not expressed it through a phone call, letter, e-mail, or visit, you have missed one of life's great honors. Plus, you may be emotionally constipated. No wonder you feel miserable. Let the gratitude out or it will hurt you.

2. *Take control of the things you actually do have control over.* There is precious little in the course of life on planet earth that we have any control over. We convince ourselves we are keeping everything locked down tight with all our lists and schedules and plans. But anyone who has ever been at the mercy of the weather at an airport will tell you that control is all an illusion. Yet there are a *few* things we do have control over. One is our thought life. We are the only ones who can change the tapes that play over and over in our head. In the New Testament, Paul refers to this discipline as "taking captive" every thought in order to make it "obedient to Christ" (2 Corinthians 10:5). This is nothing more than cultivating the

ability to dismiss thoughts that have no place in our heads (these would include doubt, irrational fear, self-loathing, hatred) and replacing them with thoughts that center on the things that are true, noble, right, pure, lovely, admirable, excellent, and praiseworthy (see Philippians 4:8). The Scriptures also teach us that as a (wo)man thinks, so is (s)he (see Proverbs 23:7, AMP). And, if you are what you think about, wouldn't you prefer to *be* Paul's list?

You can also resolve to take control over your peace. The prophet Isaiah declared that Jesus would come to earth to be our "Wonderful Counselor, Mighty God, Everlasting Father, Prince of Peace" (Isaiah 9:6). It is so easy to give others access to something that was never meant to be available for them to mess with. That is why it is called "keeping" your peace. Only you can keep it, and this is a decision that must be made ahead of time. You can't wait until you're under severe pressure and then try to hold on to peace. Instead, practice believing at the start of each day that the peace of Christ will rule (take sovereign authority, be the sole ruler) in your heart and that your personal peace is secured.

3. *Take notice.* It occurs to me that a million or more miracles occur in the natural and supernatural realms every single day. How many of these do I witness? Not very many, mainly because I am so busy doing stuff instead of being aware of the wonder of each moment.

This is not to say that I expect every moment to be a freshly mowed field with a picnic lunch (think of the chiggers!) but that my eyes are open and ready to see the ordinary miracles right in front of me. Appreciate the sounds, the smells, the tastes of this season. Open your heart and eyes to the wonder.

4. *Take your leave.* If you are someone who has a blossoming career and are tempted to skip the holidays and stay at work instead, don't! Your work is a means to an end, not an end in itself. Your life is more than your job, and if you don't take your leave, your mind will. We all need a break, so take it.

   If you are a mother who works at home, take your leave, too. For you this might mean escaping the house for a long, solitary walk and carving out some time to rest your mind from the constant communication that is the buzz of a family hive. Scripture records there were many times Jesus got alone to have some intense downtime with His Father. He would get His disciples to drop Him off somewhere desolate or get away on a boat. He did not apologize or make excuses for His need to chill out and refresh. Neither should we.

5. *Take a new direction.* I can just hear the adventurous spirits chiming, "Yes! I can't wait to do that!" and the more structured souls saying, "Now, hold up, girl." But this is a wonderful time of year to shake things up a little (by this, I do *not* mean making unilateral pronounce-

ments at the next family gathering!). I'm talking about the choice to do a new thing—or to do an old thing in a new way. Growth necessitates change. Another verse in Isaiah says, "See, I am doing a new thing! Now it springs up; do you not perceive it?" (Isaiah 43:19). We are in relationship with an infinitely creative God. Do you believe that His creative force stopped when the heavens, earth, and inhabitants were all done? He is creating on your behalf moment by moment and brings new life in unexpected places. All He asks is, "Are you looking? Do you perceive this new thing that is arising in your life? Are you willing to be in on this?"

This Christmas I invite you to give *and* take.

nutcrackers
and other strange
traditions

My son Austin has a collection of about a hundred nut-crackers. We started buying them for him when he was only a couple of years old because they look like soldiers and he was fixated on military stuff as a child. He loved toy swords and guns and playing with anything that involved defending the perimeter. His older brother Calvin and Calvin's friends would convince Austin that if they locked him up in the fort, he could stay there and guard it. They would leave him there for hours, but he was a good soldier, and a good soldier never complains.

There is a definite connection between boys and their toy soldiers. One of my husband's favorite childhood Christmas stories to recount was about the Christmas Eve that he talked his little brother, Joel, into sneaking out of the bedroom and reporting on what was under the tree. Joel has never turned down an opportu-nity at reconnaissance and crawled on his belly to see what might be waiting for the kids. When Joel got back to the bedroom, he started describing the tanks that were this high and the gigantic helicopters and the soldiers that were as big as he was. John's eyes glazed over and rolled back in his head as he imagined the military toys waiting under that tree. The next morning, he ran into the living room expecting a scene out of *Patton*. Instead, he saw the regular-sized GI Joes and accessories. That marked the end of Joel's spy days.

One Christmas tradition showcases the toy soldier. The ballet of *The Nutcracker* is an annual season standard for many families. They see it as an element of beauty and culture, and it just wouldn't be Christmas without their Nutcracker fix. I have been to see it only once. I tore my contact lens on the way there and was forced to watch it through my one good eye. Because I was down one eyeball, maybe I got only half the impact. That may be why I really don't get it at all. What kind of a godfather gives a little girl a kitchen implement in the shape of a boy's toy? And any girl who's ever had a pesky brother could predict he was going to break it (no surprise plot twist there). What about the seven-headed Mouse King? Wouldn't you say that Clara might need some analysis? And just what are they dancing about? A bad dream about rats? How did a ballet about nightmares become a Christmas standard? By the way, what exactly are sugarplum fairies, and do they dance because they are hyped up on sugar? Or do they dance because they know they will rot teeth and usher in the jig of the tooth fairy? I believe there may be a Fairy Conspiracy here.

Our family has many Christmas traditions (doesn't every family?). They all started out innocently enough—usually with a simple statement like, "Hey, I've got an idea!" That's why you have to carefully consider your choices of new activities every year because if your family likes it, it becomes an instant "tradition" and you will have to repeat it for the next forty years.

Take Christmas stockings, for example, which are a big deal at our house. The stuffing of the stockings with many small things that are personal to each family member is something that John and I have enjoyed for years. The kids tell us that their stockings are their favorite part of Christmas and that we could dispense with the rest of the gifts, but we're fairly sure they are bluffing.

It doesn't hurt that our stockings are hand-knit by my aunt Gerri. She is the family knitter (every family needs one), and she started her own tradition of knitting a Christmas stocking for each of the family kids. She might have thought better about it now, as my mom has eight brothers and sisters, and they have many children and grandchildren. But apparently we had our kids before Aunt Gerri ran out of steam, so we have the stretchy yarn stockings that will accommodate almost anything up to the size of a guitar amp (we've already tried it—too big). So by the time we stuff the stockings full of all manner of favorite snacks and Starbucks gift cards, CDs, bottles of Martinelli's Sparkling Cider, and assorted silly stuff, you would be amazed at their expandability. It almost makes you feel sorry for people who have the traditional velvet ones—they just don't know what they're missing. (Although, when I think of the amounts of time and creativity it takes to fill our stretchy knit stockings, the little velvet ones might be a tradition we'd do well to consider.)

We also have Christmas Eve traditions. One is the Stay in

Your Room Most of the Afternoon Doing Your Last-Minute Wrapping tradition. We also shower, eat something light, and go to a Christmas Eve service at a church near our home. When we come back, we sit in the living room with the fireplace going and talk about such deep, spiritual issues as:

- "Why do you think there's always one person in the handbell choir who was a late addition and can't really keep up?"
- "Was that pastor wearing a really bad toupee?"
- "Do you think candles in the hands of nine-year-old boys are a great idea?"

We allow our kids to open one Christmas Eve gift each. When they were smaller, we insisted we pick the gift they open (it was rigged since we knew we had purchased new pj's for them and they were still in the original packaging—unwashed—and it's no wonder our kids were itchy on Christmas morning).

One year we had a truly brilliant idea. We heard of a friend of ours who, in order to teach self-control to her children, got them only three presents each. Her reasoning was that was all Jesus got from the wise men. In her plan, each child would receive one present that he wanted, one that he needed, and one that was a surprise. I was trying to figure out the correlation to the Magis's gifts (Would myrrh be the need, frankincense the want, and gold the surprise?). We soon gave up on that plan because it required too much thought.

Our kids have their own tradition of sleeping in the same room on Christmas Eve. I think this one started when they were small and we were trying to think of a way to keep them from crashing the Christmas tree too early. We reasoned that corralling them in one bedroom would work better than trying to keep them in three separate rooms. This plan has now backfired on us, as they stay up talking until all hours of the morning and aren't ready to come out for Christmas morning festivities until sometime around noon. Now *we're* the ones begging to get the day started. Like I said, be careful what becomes a tradition.

One menu item for Christmas has roots in my Texas upbringing. We always eat breakfast burritos. For the uninitiated, these are flour tortillas filled with scrambled eggs, sausage, cheese, sour cream, and salsa. They are warm, spicy, and cause us to burst forth with "Feliz Navidad" as we lamely fake the other words in that chorus. In those silly "only-our-family-has-a-clue-why-we-are-laughing-so-hard" moments, you know that all the strange traditions you were *not* careful about starting are totally worth it.

Besides, nothing says "Feliz Navidad!" like breakfast burrito Christmas morning breath.

food fashionistas

It must be difficult to date a supermodel around Christmastime. Most guys would feel lucky to be dating one anytime, but during the holiday season would be a different story. You must take her to parties. Sure, she's gonna look great on your arm, as she has no lumps of any sort to ruin the design lines of the dress, but will she graciously eat your Aunt Edna's cheese log? Absolutely not. And when it comes time to dance, will she? No way. Because she did not partake of the cheese log, she has only enough energy to walk a few feet, pout, pivot, and walk back. That is what a supermodel does. I've never understood what constitutes the "super" part of supermodel. Do they excel in the pivoting? Are their pores super small? Do their bodies refuse to grow inappropriate hair? And what exactly do you get a supermodel for Christmas? She already gets free designer clothes, free jewelry, free shoes, free makeup and perfume. Spa regimens? De rigueur. Maybe she'd be super excited to receive an electronic calorie counter that doesn't exceed double digits.

I, myself, am a Supper Model. If you can't trust a skinny cook, consider me your close confidante.

Our family has not found a food category that it cannot get into other than haute cuisine. We appreciate the look of it, but if you need filling up, it ain't gonna happen with the haute stuff. I know that small, tasty, beautifully presented food is an art form in itself, but we come from Southern roots. This heritage informs us of these facts:

1. If it is sweet, salty, or fried, it's good.
2. If there's a lot of it, it's good.
3. If it's sweet, salty, and fried, *and* there's a lot of it, it's perfect.

These rules are not in line with the recommendations from the American Heart Association or the FDA Food Pyramid Chart, and we don't eat like that *all* the time; it is just our standard for what constitutes "good" food.

I noticed they recently changed the recommended servings for fruits and vegetables from five servings per day to nine. Nine! I had to ask a friend of mine who is a nutritionist how a person could eat nine apples in one day. She informed me that a "serving" is a half-cup of a fruit or vegetable. So I guess if I had a cup of collard greens with a cup of *corn*bread, a cup of fried green tomatoes, a cup of fried okra and a slice of onion, I would have to eat only one apple to achieve food pyramid perfection. That's doable.

Because I speak and perform in different cities almost every week, my husband and I get to experience a good deal of regional cuisines, and we love the variety. We have several places we have deemed "the best" at certain things. In my humble opinion, you might want to try these:

BEST PINEAPPLE SHAKE: Carl's Frozen Custard,
    Fredericksburg, Virginia
BEST FRIED CATFISH: Jerry's Catfish, Richland,
    Mississippi
BEST SCHNITZEL: The Bavarian Chef, Charlottesville,
    Virginia
BEST TEX-MEX: La Parilla, Marietta, Georgia
BEST CHICKEN SALAD: Friends & Company, Brandon,
    Mississippi
BEST SWEET TEA: My mom's house, Acworth, Georgia

Our family loves everything about a meal, other than the cleanup. We like thinking about it and questing for the right ingredients. We actually have well-defined opinions about whether the celery tastes better slant-sliced or cut straight across. We like the smell of food when it's in the oven. We like the anticipation of what it's gonna taste like when it comes out. We like discussing what we could have done to improve it *while we are eating it.* We like talking about how good it was after we're done. We like thinking about when we are going to have it again. We are all about the food.

Our family is the only family I know of that engages in

"defensive eating." We eat defensively to (1) ward off the threat of potential upcoming hunger, and (2) keep someone else from eating something that we project he *may want to eat sometime in the future* and we would then be deprived of eating ourselves.

Hence, we have some food "issues." And our cuisine-oriented idiosyncrasies tend to become more personal and strident during the holiday season.

I have friends who want to try out wonderful new recipes for Thanksgiving and Christmas. They tear them out of magazines or bring them home from parties and try to convince their families this new recipe will really knock their socks off. Can I just save you some trouble and tell you what your family will not tell you? *Nobody wants to try your new recipe.* The holidays are not the time to be experimenting. Your family wants the same stuff they've been eating for the past twenty holidays. They want comfort. They want to relive their holiday memories. Sameness is not just preferred, it's essential. If you mess with the taste, you are messing with their memories. Do not deviate from the tried and true, even if you *know for a fact* that this recipe will taste better. It's tradition or mutiny, I tell you.

We have some rock-solid menu items that will not be omitted without the threat of Death to the Cooks. These include fresh fruit salad (no nuts, no coconut), pimento-cheese-stuffed celery, turkey, cornbread dressing, cranberry sauce, sweet potato casserole, green bean casserole, dill dip with carrots (notice that I didn't list it the other way around as the dip is the main course and the carrot is the delivery agent by which the dip arrives at one's lips). There must be pumpkin, apple, and pecan pies, or else it is not The Holidays.

My mom's twin sister, Faye, makes a cookie that is out of this world. It is called a Date Nut Chew. I realize the name may sound like an activity provided for head cases by a matchmaking service, but this is a deliciously irresistible cookie filled with pieces of sweet dates and crunchy pecans. We take them up to our bedroom and hide them to protect them from the less appreciative palates.

And we are all foodies in our family. By that I am referring to the fact that every family member has favorite foods, and if you are known for hoarding certain food items, you just might receive that as one of your Christmas gifts. Last year Austin wrapped up two boxes of Captain Crunch for his dad and put them under the tree. John couldn't have been happier if he had unwrapped diamond cuff links. And the Captain Crunch was infinitely more useful than rarely worn jewelry.

When Austin was about six years old, he asked for several food items for Christmas. These included (I should have kept his list) a summer sausage of his own, special crackers and cheese, Ritz Bitz, and Capri Sun drinks. One of our family friends commented that someone needed to feed the boy. But they just did not understand the gift status of food amongst true foodies.

Elyse received a twelve-pack case of pitted black olives when she was five years old. This was during the phase when she would stick one on the end of each fingertip and then eat them off one at a time. I think she may have burned herself out on them, though, as she isn't too fond of olives now. She moved to a whole new category this year. For Christmas, she actually asked for and received a box of Styrofoam cups — the ones like you get at a deli for your tea. With this she also got a box of lids and straws for said Styrofoam cups. When she uses them, she can fix her deli-at-home drink and nurse it for hours at a time as the Styrofoam keeps it super cold and doesn't sweat like other glasses. I do not lie when I tell you that she loved that gift as much as any other.

Of course, all this food frenzy makes for a few extra pounds to deal with every January, but I have noticed in the magazines that the trend for next year is something called The Shrunken Jacket.

That would be every jacket in my closet that fit last year. Sometimes food issues make you fashion savvy after all.

squirrels
up the
family tree

It may be harder to find for your spouse a gift that says it all than for anyone else on your list. I mean, it's really difficult to find something that adequately says, "You are The One, my everything. I love you devotedly."

I've tried. It's hard.

Year before last, I thought I had finally found The Gift—something that expressed my husband's penchants and would be a source of unending pleasure for him. No, not edible underwear. I found him The Squirrel Defender Bird Feeder.

In order to appreciate my enthusiasm, you have to know just how much my husband despises squirrels. It must be genetic, since his dad has a very distinct hatred of them, too. The furry creatures with the fluffy tails engender such a dramatic response in John and his dad that I believe it must be tied to some instinctual predator reaction. They believe that squirrels are out to undermine their dominion of their yards. We actually bought John's dad a sweatshirt with squirrels posed for mug shots and a description of them as if they were most-wanted criminals. Such is the Renfroe Gene Code.

John also feeds a variety of birds in our backyard and cannot *stand* the fact that squirrels will swing from his feeders, spilling the birdseed in their attempts to get some of it into their furry little bellies. This causes my husband's blood pressure to rise at least fifteen points. So this bird feeder, which had a motorized ring around the bottom that was guaranteed to start circling the moment any squirrel dared to venture onto it (like when someone got pitched off the merry-go-round in first grade), was found treasure. The box it came in even had a cartoon rendering of people standing around holding their sides from the hilarious sight of a squirrel being flung while the birds dined in peace. I had happened upon the perfect husband gift.

Unfortunately, I didn't read the fine print. Seems the thing must be regularly charged to keep the slinger a-slingin' and it can't distinguish between skinny squirrels and fat doves. The doves didn't think it was funny at all. I also failed to factor in that squirrels are curiously fast learners and after being slung only twice would refuse to go anywhere near the thing. I saith unto thee, The Squirrel Slinger failed to deliver the never-ending joy it promised.

I know there are people who come to Matthew's opening chapter of the New Testament and give a heartfelt yawn. You know the part I'm talking about: In my Bible, the heading states, "The Genealogy of Jesus." Yawns abound except from those people in your family who love to trace their roots. In this passage, they find spiritual impetus to continue their quest to dig up more info on the family history. I'll tell you what you'll find if you dig long enough in the family tree. You will find squirrels: the people you would rather not be related to. But you don't get to pick who you're related to, do ya?

Jesus had squirrels in his family tree, and I am thankful the Bible doesn't attempt to airbrush them out of there. Let's list a few, shall we?

- Abraham — sure, he was the father of our faith, but in his doubt of God's protection, he claimed that his wife was his sister and almost messed the whole thing up
- Jacob — a trickster and thief
- Rahab — a prostitute who was redeemed from her lifestyle
- Tamar — another girl who wasn't actually a harlot but just pretended to be one in order to seduce her father-in-law (after she was widowed and her brother-in-law refused to sleep with her — God killed him for it, too. It's all right there in Genesis 38. Obviously, the world got off to a rocky start.)
- David — a great king with adultery, murder, and incest under his own roof

Sounds like a great bunch of folks to have at the family gathering, right?

Please tell me that by now you know that *every* family has squirrelly types. No family is immune. I tell my kids that all families look normal until you spend a single holiday with them. The squirrelliness *will* reveal itself. There are family members who know just how to push your buttons. They have been students of your buttons. They may have even manufactured some of your buttons. They are responsible for your uncontrollable twitches every time you consider going home for the holidays. And during the season of peace on earth, you drive to the family gathering with white knuckles and heart palpitations, recalling the last holiday fiasco and dreading the inevitable eruption that comes out of left field just as you are congratulating yourself on navigating the day without incident.

Do I overstate, or is someone feelin' me out there?

Isn't it interesting that the holy-days can bring to the surface some of the most decidedly un-holy feelings about the people who have known us longest and best? Maybe it's the knowledge that they also know us at our worst. Whatever the case, they are family, and we are bound by blood or marriage to figure out how to relate to them with love and grace in the emotional pressure cooker that is associated with The Holiday Season. As many cherished memories as we have with them, we probably have a secret stash of disappointments and inexplicable flash reactions up our emotional sleeves.

I recall a Christmas holiday in our own household a few years back after Calvin had gone away to college. When that first child leaves, the family dynamic shifts and everyone is left to sort out the new roles. Austin, our secondborn, had come to enjoy his newfound status as King of the Basement and was also truck-sharing with Calvin while Calvin was away at college. (It's sort of like a time-share, only there are wheels involved.) They had been sniping at each other for several days leading up to the incident that caused much junk from longtime testosterone/sibling stuff to bubble to the surface and overflow into an angry exchange that contained phrases like:

"You always _____."
"I can't believe that you _____."
"You're never gonna change."
"Remember that time he _____?"

There was shouting involved, and I had had enough. I took all three of my kids into the office and sat them down (at the time they were nineteen, sixteen, and thirteen). Elyse was included, too, as there's no need to have a family powwow without the whole family. My speech fell along the lines that they had taken the emotional equivalent of a Polaroid snapshot of their sibling at a certain age and attached the old feelings that came with that snapshot. Because of that, they were stuck relating to each other in ways that were no longer accurate. I told my kids that if the natural order prevailed, they would be brothers and sister a good deal longer than John and I would be their parents.

As I left the room, I said, "You *will* sit in this room and peel this onion until there is resolution and forgiveness and a new way of relating to each other." And they knew I meant it. I am a firm believer in letting your kids work stuff out.

About an hour later, they emerged having sorted through why they reacted to each other in such knee-jerk ways. There was forgiveness asked for and given, and they laid out a new path for themselves and committed to try to see the best in each other instead of the obsolete mental Polaroids.

But that's hard, isn't it? For some of us, the mental image isn't a matter of simply tossing the Polaroid; it's more like erasing an epic movie or sandblasting something hurtful that seems chiseled in stone. What's a damaged heart to do?

I believe that Paul addresses this subject in his second letter to the Corinthians. One of my favorite verses concerning the renovation that happens in the human heart when Jesus comes to occupy it is 2 Corinthians 5:17, which states, "Therefore, if anyone is in Christ, he is a new creation; the old has gone, the new has come!" There is even an exclamation point to let us know that this is a pretty amazing concept. Out with the old, in with the new! Woo-hoo! I've been forgiven completely and can do my happy-ever-after dance and celebrate.

If only this is where the passage stopped. Let me give you "the rest of the story" as it is paraphrased in *The Message* Bible:

> All this comes from the God who settled the relationship between us and him, and then called us to settle our relationships with each other. God put the world square with himself through the Messiah, giving the world a fresh start by offering forgiveness of sins. God has given us the task of telling everyone what he is doing. We're Christ's representatives. God uses us to persuade men and women to drop their differences and enter into God's work of making things right between them. We're speaking for Christ himself now: Become friends with God; he's already a friend with you. (2 Corinthians 5:18-20)

This presents a twist to our happy-ever-after dance, doesn't it? It seems, according to Paul's line of reasoning, that reconciliation never was meant to be something we received from God only and then kept all for ourselves. Nope. Paul tells us we have now been handed this gift to pass around like there's no tomorrow. In fact, that would be a good way to look at it.

- What if there's no tomorrow?
- With whom would you reconcile if you knew this was your last day on earth?
- What phone call would you make?
- Would you write an e-mail or go visit in person?
- How far would you drive? Would you hop a plane to make it right between you?
- Could you release that grudge you've been nursing for these many years? Could you ask for or offer forgiveness? Or has your heart become hard?

Sometimes we have these issues of unforgiveness and anger and, quite frankly, it's been going on for so long that we sometimes can't even recall quite how it all started. We just know that we have "good reason" not to embrace this squirrelly person.

I say to us all, with scriptural support: "We don't have the right."

As Americans, we have made a religion out of our rights. I am thankful we have so many rights that are precious to us, but as people who have received the unconditional forgiveness that God has offered us through Jesus, we no longer have the right to any unforgiveness of our own. How incredibly arrogant of us to believe that any offense we have been dealt could even begin to rival that of God's hurt at our rejection of Him and our litany of sins against Him? That would be equivalent to our saying, "Thanks, God, for forgiving me of my many sins, but You really don't understand the kind of hurt I've suffered in this relationship. I appreciate that You dropped Your grudge against me and offered me eternal life because of Your commitment to reconciliation, but if it's all the same to you, I'm gonna need to hold on to this offense." Aren't we, in essence, saying, "I'm more important than You, God"?

Paul says that we have now been passed the baton of forgiveness, so to speak, and it is our privilege *and* responsibility to give up our right to be right. In the NIV, 2 Corinthians 5:18 contains the words, "(God) gave us the ministry of reconciliation." Does it surprise you to know you are a Reconciliation Minister? There is no special collar for you to wear, and you won't get preferential parking at the hospital. What you *will* get is the peace that comes from knowing you have done everything in your power to extend the same grace that was extended to you.

You will also have the joy of sending your emotional Polaroids to the spiritual shredder and have space in your heart's photo album for a whole new page.

picture this

Christmas is a veritable feast for photoholics. They will take pictures of any and all moments, candid or posed. They believe it is their familial mandate to chronicle the good, the bad, and the ugly for us to recall for years to come. I prefer my soft-focus misty watercolor memories of "the way we were," but the family photographers want it all on film *in Technicolor*, complete with red-eye shots.

I remember a few years back when the feature du jour of the latest cameras was the flash that flashed twice to "fake off" your pupils before it actually snapped the picture on the third flash. In this tricky way, the red-eye phenomenon would be defeated. The actual result of this flash feature was that many people prematurely relaxed their smile and we got many very sad-looking photos of friends and family. And have you noticed that the Red-Eye-in-Your-Christmas-Photos syndrome plagues only the lighter-eye-color crowd? You will have nine people in a shot and only the two who have blue or green eyes will look like demon spawn. They

have photo-fix software to exorcise the red, but if you aren't careful, you can end up with a pupil on your forehead.

I know there are people for whom the idea of photos being dis-
organized or unmounted brings on fits of stress-induced asthma,
but in our immediate family, we do not have scrapbooks, or even
photo albums for that matter. Well, let me clarify that. We do have
photo albums. They sit empty in the chest that has all the loose
photos in it. That's right. We have a big old steamer trunk with
all our pictures in plastic bins inside it. Not only that but with
the advent of scanners at every Walgreens, we even threw away
our kajillion envelopes of photo negatives. The scrapbookers are
puffing on their inhalers right now at the thought of my precious
family photos languishing in the basement, but I prefer to think
of it as my deference to future daughters-in-law. I would not want
to be so bold as to assume that my version of history is the defini-
tive one.

Have you ever stopped to consider how many photo albums
your picture is in? In other countries? Think about it. How many
times have you been going about your business here in the good
ol' U. S. of A. and inadvertently walked past some foreign tourists
as they are snapping off some shots? You are probably in the background of hundreds of such photos over the course of your life. So
even if you think you're the type who avoids the camera, somewhere
in the world, someone may be digitally cropping you out of their
picture.

Photo editing technology can also assist us in righting an injus-
tice that has been done. In most families, the photoholic is always

behind the camera and never in the holiday pictures. His determination to preserve the moment for future generations means that *he may never be seen* by future generations. Thanks to Photoshop, we can insert him. Just because his image won't exactly match what's taking place in the photo (for example, all the relatives are out on a sleigh ride, photoholic is edited in from his sole existing shot—the July Fourth barbecue where he is wearing shorts and flip-flops) doesn't mean he doesn't belong in the picture.

I have only a handful of photos of my kids with Santa—or any other costumed figures, for that matter. The boys were not really interested in them, and Elyse was much afraid of anything in a suit (Chuck E Cheese was the stuff of nightmares for her). We have only a couple of pictures with our children in Christmas attire at all. When my kids were small, you had to order your Christmas Greeting Card photos by October 1 in order to have them back from the printer in time to send out for the holidays. Nowadays you can print your cards off on your own computer, but back then you had to purchase your Christmas outfits nine months in advance (that took major trig calculations to predict what size your kids would be by the next fall), convince them that matching Christmas outfits were not effeminate, bribe them with promises of Hot Wheels and candy, and then get them to look delightfully angelic after missing with the hairspray and accidentally spraying it in their eyes. We just never thought the yearly family Christmas photo was quite worth the grief.

Thanks to Photoshop, you can import your kids onto any background, whittle ten pounds off your middle, give your husband a more prominent chin line and a less receding hairline, change the print on your outfits, and *voila!* Painless Christmas Photo done!

The question we must address today is this: At what age is it appropriate for children to balk at the insistence of their parents making them take a picture with the mall-variety Santa Claus?

Exhibit A: A friend of mine receives a Christmas card every year from a fine, upstanding family here in Georgia. When she first began receiving their family Christmas photo (more than two decades ago), the boys were small and the photos of them with Santa were fun. Now these boys are well into their thirties, with wives and young families of their own. One is in medical school, and the other is an executive with a bright future, but they still pose every year (at their mother's insistence) for their brotherly photo with Santa.

What say you? Cute, or just plain sick?

All I know is that my boys would do it only on a dare, and then only if we promised that the photo would end up in the steamer trunk in the basement.

ho, ho,
home
improvements

When I went to Graceland a couple of years ago, I learned many interesting facts about Elvis. One that stands out in my memory was the fact that Elvis never allowed anyone except his close friends and family members to go to the upstairs portion of his home. If you wanted to see Elvis, you had to wait downstairs. Having had a few holiday open houses myself, I see the wisdom in the Elvis Rule.

An open house is a good idea taken to an illogical extreme. It is, indeed, a good thing to hospitably welcome people into your home. It is not, however, a good idea to give a group of people a free pass to look in all your closets and poke around your home like it's a museum. If only we had velvet ropes to establish boundaries.

When we were on church staff, we used to open our home to the entire congregation one night around the holidays. We would prepare all sorts of food and clean the house until we were in a tizzy. All this so that we could stand and welcome many people while trying to keep from passing out due to cleaning-induced fatigue. But at least we could boast that we accomplished a lot. It was a great excuse to get the house spic and span and decorated in record time.

I seem to have a special holiday-related affliction similar to S.A.D. (Seasonal Affective Disorder), where people get inordinately depressed because they don't receive enough sunlight. I get something called R.A.D. (Remodeling Affective Disorder). This is a mental disorder that propels type A, driven people to do all the household projects they have been meaning to do all year in the last quarter of the year, spurred on by the guarantee of having company over the holidays. A built-in deadline is imposed if we must get it all done before the open-housers and relatives arrive.

If there were drugs to stop this insanity, my husband would have already bought stock in the company. Unfortunately, he is the one who gets stuck executing my "unique and artistic" ideas (read: "no instructions available") while he is desperately needing to finish his own decorating for the holidays. You can cut the potential conflict with a putty knife.

In our twenty-two-plus-year marriage, we have come to accept many of our differences and have actually learned to appreciate them, but in our approaches to problem solving, we have distinctly opposite preferences about how you reach resolution. I want to talk, talk, talk it out. I want to talk about the way we are talking about it or why he isn't talking about it. He just wants to leave the room and think about it. He knows that this makes me feel as though he is walking out on the discussion, so he will stay in the room and just not say anything. According to his rationale, his silence ends the discussion. What most men fail to realize is that the discussion is most definitely *not* over. It has merely changed venues. Instead of being out in the open air, where he would have a chance to present his perspective, the argument has merely *changed venues* to the inside of my head, where I have now not only internalized my side of things but also turned him into a mental sock puppet as I rattle off what I *imagine* he would say if he were speaking. Consequently, after several moments of silence, I can actually be *more* upset than when he was talking for himself because I have already jumped to twenty-seven conclusions based on what I imagined he might say. I wonder if men will ever understand this about the female mind.

But the need to tackle household projects during the holidays may be one arena in our marriage where John has decided to just go with the strangeness, as it eventually works to the good of the household (if he can survive it). Besides, any excuse to spend time at Home Depot beats no excuse. I've figured out that hardware stores are the non-drinker's bar. All the guys there know your name. And they're really glad you came. It's good for John's ego, too. He told me that every time he goes down the laser stud finder aisle, they all point to him as he walks by.

This year the home-improvement plan got a little more involved than either of us envisioned, and I must say that my stud of a husband proved heroic. When my friends talk about being "into rocks," they are talking about diamonds. When I talk about being "into rocks," I am referring to big stones that you can dig up out of the ground. As of late, I have been requesting that John create all sorts of things out of them. I think it makes me feel more connected to the area of central Texas where I grew up. He made me a rock waterfall and patio in the backyard. Then I thought we needed to move the rock creativity indoors—all the way into our bedroom.

I don't know where I came up with this idea, but I wanted to take out the carpet in our bedroom and have John lay a random tile floor. This made perfect sense in my mind's eye. There would be tiles of varying shades and sizes so that the floor would look unique and artisan-ish. When we went to the tile store to quest for said tiles, there was a dreadful math word problem awaiting me. Remember when we were in fifth grade and got hit with the sort of word problem that read, "If John is going to lay a random tile floor for his nutsy wife and the room is 14' by 24', will he need tile sizes that are divisible by 3 inches or by 4 inches?" This was my idea of living hell. Fortunately, there were many males standing around, ready to perform feats of math magic. After much scratching of heads, we decided to go with the tiles that were multiples of three. Then the next level of math commenced to cipher the total area as it relates to the differing sizes of the stones divisible by 3. It was a math marathon. This was a nightmarish component I had not foreseen in my "random" and "artisan" visions.

So my man trucked the tiles home and started the weeklong process of removing the old carpet, laying the subfloor for two whole days (this also was not on my vision list), and then we started the portion that would bring this glorious Tuscan floor to fruition: the laying of the tile. It was hard—really hard. In my commitment to randomness, the tiles I chose were of different thicknesses, so John had to carefully level every one to match the one next to it. This process took two days and much staring to make sure that no two similar pieces were side by side.

By the time the floor was finished and grouted, John had literally worked his buns off. I am not exaggerating. They're gone and may never make a comeback. As we have aged, we've developed a scale that represents how many anti-inflammatory agents we have to ingest to bring a project to completion. We call it The Celebrex Factor. This floor scored off that chart. But my beautiful Italian tile floor looks mah-velous, and we are positive that it is one of a kind. When John finished and saw how great it looked, I asked him if he would ever do it for money. He shook his head and replied, "Only for love." Now if I could just get him to agree to make our bedroom complete with the installation of a chocolate fountain. He has agreed in theory, but he made me promise that he can wait until his Valentine's Affective Disorder kicks in.

you must be present to win

I was online a few years before my husband decided the Internet was a necessary evil and he must learn to surf. It took him a little while to get the hang of the mouse, and typing is a two-finger activity for him. This made for some very slow Web trawling, but he eventually got the hang of it.

While trying not to lord my Internet savvy over him (bad form), I walked into the office many times to see him registering online for various giveaways. Some of these were the ones we all know and love, such as Publisher's Clearinghouse. (What *is* a Publisher's Clearinghouse, anyway? Is that where old publishers go to find new jobs? If so, how do they have so much money to give away?) Other lesser-known contest sites (EZSweeps, Click and Win!, Win-o-rama) also grabbed John's attention and personal information. His rationale was that *someone* had to win, and he wasn't even using a postage stamp to get the job done.

What my Internet novice husband was not catching on to was that each time he filled out his information to "register to win," the companies were harvesting his e-mail address to sell to Internet marketing companies. Poor guy. He thought he was gonna get us a cool million for free, but all he got was five years' worth of junk e-mails every day. You wouldn't believe (or maybe you would if you've signed up for all that, too) the amount of spam advertisements he gets. I think if you strung them all together, you would get a subject line that said, "Lose Weight While You Pay Less for Ink Cartridges and Get Your Degree Online So You Can Be Your Own Boss and Refinance Your House Before Interest Rates Go Up Again and Then You'll Pay Too Much for Your Pain Meds." You know you have some in your inbox, too.

My registration temptation is slightly different. I sign up only for things that have cardboard boxes that you drop your registration slip into. I love sliding my slip of contact information through that slit in the top. If it's a drawing where they need you to stay around for the whole event, they'll put those six words at the bottom of the registration slip that make you think twice about entering: "You must be present to win." I can't tell you how many times I have filled in all my pertinent information only to see those six words and decide I was not going to stay around long enough for the drawing so I might as well not even enter the contest. It is a qualifier of sorts.

"You must be present to win."

How can we "win" this Christmas? Wouldn't it be great to enter into the season anticipating a bouquet of standout moments that will become treasured memories? How about intentionally and purposefully planning to be an agent of encouragement and blessing to each person in your circle of influence?

"You must be present to win."

I believe that those six words, if taken to heart, could alter your perception and experience of this holy, zany season.

First, we must be present, fully engaged, in the moments that are happening in our lives as they are happening. We all have difficulties with this practice. I know I do. If you were to pick a series of random moments in my day (ones during which I am awake) and freeze the action of that moment and then access my thoughts that were occurring at that moment, I could pretty much assure you I would not really be there. I am ashamed to admit it, but it's true.

At any given moment, we are all tempted to check out of the present and allow our minds to wander backward into the past to something we wish we could change (a mistake, a wrong choice, a sad occurrence) or forward into an area we are worried about (health, relationships, finances). All this time that our mind is distracted by the past (no going back) or the future (can't predict it), there are amazing miracles that go unnoticed because we are not really p-r-e-s-e-n-t. And it's a moment-to-moment choice to live in the here and now.

Our family learned this very painfully a few years ago. My dad was diagnosed with pancreatic cancer when he was only fifty-eight. When we received the results in late March, it was already in his liver and the doctors declared it inoperable. We knew that barring a miracle (which we believed was entirely possible), Dad's time on earth was short. We prayed and hoped, and we learned to clear the deck of our lives and celebrate every day. It's interesting that when faced with such a difficult reality, we had no problem deciding what was worth our time and what wasn't. We knew that every day with Dad was to be treasured because there was a very limited supply. (If only we would remember that this is true for *all* of us, sick or healthy.)

I wish I could tell you that the lessons of that poignant time were so powerful that I no longer have an issue with being fully present in the life God has blessed me with, but that would not be true. I still drift. I still find myself mentally and emotionally a million miles away from the people and situations that *are* my life. But my heart's desire is to be fully present with each breath so that I don't miss the measure of joy or sorrow contained in that moment. I don't have to live in the negative loops that play in my head regarding my past. Because of the mercy of God and the gift of His Son, Jesus, I can be fully forgiven of everything wrong that I have ever done—if I just ask Him. Because of the faithfulness of God and His promise to be present in my life (to actually live in and through me!), I don't have to live in fear of the future and whether or not I will have enough, do enough, be enough. The future is ultimately beyond my control, and I can relax in the knowledge that God knows all about it. I can, you can, live in this gift called "the present."

"You must be present to win."

Might I add that you must be (the) present to win?

When my boys were younger and they would start to do the guy thing of friendly tussling, I would send them to the basement. The downstairs was always "Man Land," where the boys could be a little rougher in the absence of breakable objects. If this friendly tussling began to take on a less-than-friendly tone, I would open the basement door and shout, "Don't make me come down there!" They got the interpretation: "If you don't stop it on your own, you are not going to enjoy the consequences of my interrupting whatever I'm doing to come down there and stop it." This was usually pretty effective, except for the time Austin put a pool cue stick through Calvin's bedroom door. If I was coming down, I was *mad.*

It's hard to imagine that God would come to earth and not be mad. If I were God and had placed Adam and Eve in a perfect world with a perfect garden and a standing appointment to interface with The Creator and Sovereign Ruler of the Universe every day with one teensy stipulation to avoid the fruit of one tree and *they blew it,* I would have been mad to have had to come down here and take care of it. But that's the miracle: God wasn't mad (although I must admit that He seemed rather ticked off until He got a lot of stuff communicated through the major prophets). He just wanted things fixed. And this is what Jesus did for us. He embodied another parenting sentiment: "If you want something done right, you have to do it yourself." He was the gift of heaven. He was the present.

And so are you.

You probably cycle through the same thoughts that I do about Christmas and giving and gifts: *I want to get the perfect gift for _____, something that adequately expresses how much I love and appreciate her. It's so hard to find something like that. No matter what I get her, it's not going to be right. I am going to fail. She won't know*

how much I love her. What am I going to do? And what if she gets me
something extravagant and my gift seems measly in comparison? What
sort of loser will that make me? Why can't I figure this thing out?

Try keeping it simple: Be (the) present to win.

Be available. Be engaged. Be there with your whole heart.

Then, no matter what you wrap up and give to them, they will
know they have received the ultimate gift from you—the gift of
your love.

I promise you that if you fully engage this Christmas, it's in
the bag.

acknowledgments

There is a chapter in this book where I discuss what a gift it is for us to be able to say, "Thank you," to people who have made a difference in our life. It is with great Christmas cheer that I am able to thank some of them here.

Mondo-Incredi-Gargantuan-Uber-Buckets of Gratitude to:

Christ—without you, it would just be "-mas," and life would be useless.

My Santa, John—thank you for celebrating life with me every day. You are my favorite gift.

The Fam (Calvin, Austin, Elyse)—you guys are the reason we have all these traditions anyway. Thanks for being born to us.

Mom (the Most Competitive Farkel Player Ever)—because your birthday is on Christmas Eve eve, you will forever get fewer than your deserved quota of presents. Thank you for being such a cheerleader for all that God does in our family.

All other family members—I was *not* thinking of any of you when I wrote the "Squirrels" chapter. It was based on stories I have heard from *other* families.

Terry, Dan, Traci, Melanie, Jessica, Andrea (and the Mighty Host of Angelic Beings who are NavPress)—you are a gift to me. Thank you for believing there might be something here that might make a difference.

Beach Girls and Cheesecake Factory Posse—you support me better than my strongest underwire. Friends are cheaper than therapy.

My Destiny Family—it is good to journey together.

about the author

S he has been described as "a triple shot of espresso in a decaf world," but there really isn't a latte cup large enough to hold the high-octane vitality that Anita Renfroe brings when she unleashes her inventive blend of musical comedy and inspiration to sold-out venues across the United States. Highly original, bodacious in her faith, and unashamedly real, Anita leaves her audiences with cheeks that hurt and hearts infused with humor and hope.

She is also the author of *The Purse-Driven Life: It Really Is All About Me* and the creator of other comedy projects, available in DVD format. She makes her home in Atlanta with her hunk of burning love (John) and her three semi-grown children (Calvin, Austin, and Elyse). You can find out more than you ever wanted to know about her at www.anitarenfroe.com.

ADD SOME PURSE-ONALITY TO YOUR LIFE.